The Official Rails-to-Trails
Conservancy Guidebook

T0160363

Rail-Trail
Hall of Fame

A selection of America's premier rail-trails

2nd Edition

 WILDERNESS PRESS ... *on the trail since 1967*

Rail-Trail Hall of Fame

Maps: Lohnes+Wright; map data courtesy of Environmental Systems Research Institute
Cover design: Scott McGrew
Book design and layout: Annie Long

Library of Congress Cataloging-in-Publication Data

Names: Rails-to-Trails Conservancy.
Title: Rail-trail hall of fame.
Description: Second edition. | Birmingham, Alabama : Wilderness Press, 2020.
Identifiers: LCCN 2019057541 (print) | LCCN 2019057542 (ebook) | ISBN
    9781643590400 (paperback) | ISBN 9781643590387 (ebook)
Subjects: LCSH: Rail-trails—United States—Guidebooks. | Hiking—United States—
    Guidebooks. | Bicycle trails—United States—Guidebooks. | Outdoor recreation—
    United States—Guidebooks.
Classification: LCC GV191.4 .R34 2020 (print) | LCC GV191.4 (ebook) | DDC
    796.50973—dc23
LC record available at https://lccn.loc.gov/2019057541
LC ebook record available at https://lccn.loc.gov/2019057542

Manufactured in the United States of America

Published by: **WILDERNESS PRESS**
              An imprint of AdventureKEEN
              2204 First Ave. S, Ste. 102
              Birmingham, AL 35233
              800-443-7227; fax 877-374-9016

Visit wildernesspress.com for a complete listing of our books and for ordering information. Contact us at our website, at facebook.com/wildernesspress1967, or at twitter.com
/wilderness1967 with questions or comments. To find out more about who we are and
what we're doing, visit blog.wildernesspress.com.

Distributed by Publishers Group West

Front cover: Walkway Over the Hudson, part of the Hudson Valley Trail Network (see
page 22); photographed by Fred Schaeffer. *Back cover:* Hudson Valley Rail Trail, part of
the Hudson Valley Trail Network (see page 22); photographed by Fred Schaeffer.

SAFETY NOTICE: Although Wilderness Press and Rails-to-Trails Conservancy have
made every attempt to ensure that the information in this book is accurate at press time,
they are not responsible for any loss, damage, injury, or inconvenience that may occur to
anyone while using this book. You are responsible for your own safety and health while in
the wilderness. The fact that a trail is described in this book does not mean that it will be
safe for you. Be aware that trail conditions can change from day to day. Always check local
conditions, know your own limitations, and consult a map.

About Rails-to-Trails Conservancy

Headquartered in Washington, D.C., Rails-to-Trails Conservancy (RTC) is a nonprofit organization dedicated to creating a nationwide network of trails from former rail lines and connecting corridors to build healthier places for healthier people.

Railways helped build America. Spanning from coast to coast, these ribbons of steel linked people, communities, and enterprises, spurring commerce and forging a single nation that bridges a continent. But in recent decades, many of these routes have fallen into disuse, severing communal ties that helped bind Americans together.

When RTC opened its doors in 1986, the rail-trail movement was in its infancy. Most projects focused on single, linear routes in rural areas, created for recreation and conservation. RTC sought broader protection for the unused corridors, incorporating rural, suburban, and urban routes.

Year after year, RTC's efforts to protect and align public funding with trail building created an environment that allowed trail advocates in communities across the country to initiate trail projects. These ever-growing ranks of trail professionals, volunteers, and RTC supporters have built momentum for the national rail-trails movement. As the number of supporters multiplied, so did the rail-trails.

Americans now enjoy more than 24,000 miles of open rail-trails; as they flock to the trails to connect with family members and friends, enjoy nature, and get to places in their local neighborhoods and beyond, their economic prosperity, health, and overall well-being continue to flourish.

A signature endeavor of RTC is **TrailLink.com,** America's portal to these rail trails, as well as other multiuse trails. When RTC launched TrailLink.com in 2000, our organization was one of the first to compile such detailed trail information on a national scale. Today, the website continues to play a critical role in both encouraging and satisfying the country's growing need for opportunities to ride, walk, skate, or run for recreation or transportation. This free trail-finder database—which includes detailed descriptions, interactive maps, photo galleries, and first-hand ratings and reviews—can be used as a companion resource to the trails in this guidebook.

With a grassroots community more than 1 million strong, RTC is committed to ensuring a better future for America made possible by trails and the connections they inspire. Learn more at **railstotrails.org.**

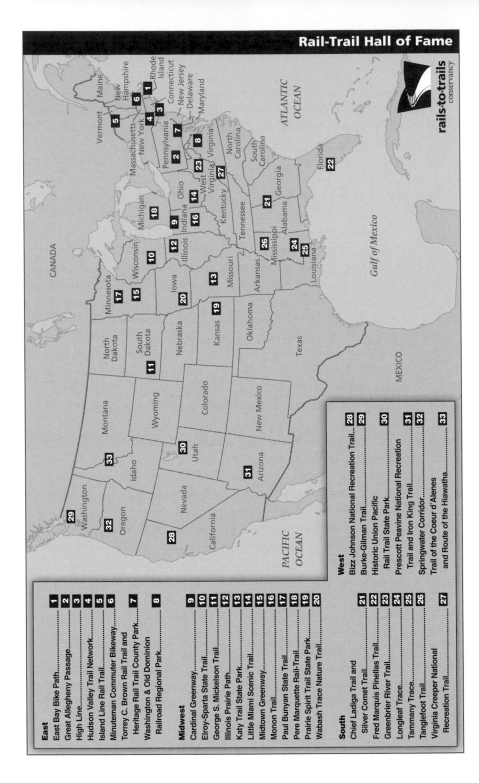

Rail-Trail Hall of Fame

rails·to·trails
conservancy

ATLANTIC OCEAN

Gulf of Mexico

PACIFIC OCEAN

MEXICO

CANADA

East
East Bay Bike Path.............................. 1
Great Allegheny Passage..................... 2
High Line... 3
Hudson Valley Trail Network............... 4
Island Line Rail Trail........................... 5
Minuteman Commuter Bikeway........... 6
Torrey C. Brown Rail Trail and
Heritage Rail Trail County Park...... 7
Washington & Old Dominion
Railroad Regional Park..................... 8

Midwest
Cardinal Greenway.............................. 9
Elroy-Sparta State Trail....................... 10
George S. Mickelson Trail.................... 11
Illinois Prairie Path............................. 12
Katy Trail State Park............................ 13
Little Miami Scenic Trail..................... 14
Midtown Greenway.............................. 15
Monon Trail... 16
Paul Bunyan State Trail....................... 17
Pere Marquette Rail-Trail................... 18
Prairie Spirit Rail State Park............... 19
Wabash Trace Nature Trail.................. 20

South
Chief Ladiga Trail and
Silver Comet Trail............................ 21
Fred Marquis Pinellas Trail................. 22
Greenbrier River Trail......................... 23
Longleaf Trace..................................... 24
Tammany Trace.................................... 25
Tanglefoot Trail................................... 26
Virginia Creeper National
Recreation Trail............................... 27

West
Bizz Johnson National Recreation Trail... 28
Burke-Gilman Trail.............................. 29
Historic Union Pacific
Rail Trail State Park......................... 30
Prescott Peavine National Recreation
Trail and Iron King Trail.................. 31
Springwater Corridor.......................... 32
Trail of the Coeur d'Alenes
and Route of the Hiawatha............... 33

Table of Contents

About Rails-to-Trails Conservancy iii

Foreword vii

Acknowledgments ix

Introduction 1

How to Use This Book 5

EAST 8

1 East Bay Bike Path 10

2 Great Allegheny Passage 14

3 High Line 18

4 Hudson Valley Trail Network 22

5 Island Line Rail Trail 28

6 Minuteman Commuter Bikeway 32

7 Torrey C. Brown Rail Trail and
   Heritage Rail Trail County Park 36

8 Washington & Old Dominion Railroad Regional Park . . 41

MIDWEST 46

9 Cardinal Greenway 48

10 Elroy-Sparta State Trail 53

11 George S. Mickelson Trail 57

12 Illinois Prairie Path 61

13 Katy Trail State Park 65

14 Little Miami Scenic Trail 69

15 Midtown Greenway 73

16 Monon Trail 77

17 Paul Bunyan State Trail 81

18 Pere Marquette Rail-Trail 85

19 Prairie Spirit Trail State Park 89

20 Wabash Trace Nature Trail 93

SOUTH 98

21 Chief Ladiga Trail and Silver Comet Trail 100

22 Fred Marquis Pinellas Trail. 104

23 Greenbrier River Trail 108

24 Longleaf Trace. 112

25 Tammany Trace. 116

26 Tanglefoot Trail 121

27 Virginia Creeper National Recreation Trail 126

WEST 130

28 Bizz Johnson National Recreation Trail. 132

29 Burke-Gilman Trail. 136

30 Historic Union Pacific Rail Trail State Park 140

31 Prescott Peavine National Recreation Trail
and Iron King Trail 144

32 Springwater Corridor. 148

33 Trail of the Coeur d'Alenes and Route of the Hiawatha . 152

Index 157

Photo Credits 164

Support Rails-to-Trails Conservancy 165

Dramatic columnar basalt lines California's Bizz Johnson National Recreation Trail (see page 132).

Foreword

Welcome to *Rail-Trail Hall of Fame*, a comprehensive companion for discovering America's top rail-trails. This guidebook will help you uncover fantastic opportunities to get outdoors on these model pathways—whether for exercise, transportation, or just pure fun.

Rails-to-Trails Conservancy's mission is to create a nationwide network of trails, just like these, to build healthier places for healthier people. We hope this book will inspire you to experience firsthand how trails can connect people to one another and to the places they love, while also creating connections to nature, history, and culture.

Since its founding in 1986, RTC has witnessed a massive growth in the rail-trail and active transportation movement. Today, more than 24,000 miles of completed rail-trails provide invaluable benefits for people and communities across the country. We hope you find this book to be a delightful and informative resource for discovering the nation's many iconic and unique trail destinations.

I'll be out on the trails, too, experiencing the thrill of the adventure right alongside you. Be sure to say hello and share your experience with us on social media! We want to hear how you #GoByTrail. You can find us @railstotrails on Facebook, Instagram, and Twitter.

See you on the trail!

Ryan Chao, President
Rails-to-Trails Conservancy

The Burke-Gilman Trail connects residents with many parks in the Seattle area (see page 136).

Acknowledgments

Special acknowledgment goes to Amy Kapp and Laura Stark, coeditors of this guidebook, and to Derek Strout for his work on the creation of the trail maps included in the book. We are also appreciative of the following contributors and trail managers we called on for assistance to ensure the maps, photographs, and trail descriptions are as accurate as possible.

Cindy Dickerson   Debra Eliezer

Brandi Horton   Jake Laughlin

Kesi Marcus

Rhode Island's East Bay Bike Path provides waterfront views of Narragansett Bay (see page 10).

Cascading blossoms fill the Virginia Creeper National Recreation Trail with beauty in the spring and summer (see page 126).

Introduction

Of the more than 2,100 rail-trails across the United States, 33 inductees have been selected for the Rail-Trail Hall of Fame and represent the country's expansive breadth and diversity. Follow this special collection of rail-trails and you will experience the lush ravines and leafy canopies of the Midwest, the gleaming skyscrapers and maritime charm of the East, the rural landscapes and rolling hills of Appalachia in the South, and the rugged and hauntingly arid beauty of the West. From sleepy small towns to bustling metropolises, sandy beaches to mountain peaks, and dense woodlands to open prairie—it's all represented here.

Rails-to-Trails Conservancy began recognizing these exemplary rail-trails—singly or in combination with others—in its Rail-Trail Hall of Fame in 2007. We select inductees on such merits as scenic value, high use, trail and trailside amenities, historical significance, excellence in management and maintenance of facility, community connections, and geographic distribution. Signs along these routes announce their inclusion in the Hall of Fame, and inductees also receive promotion on our website and in stories in our nationally distributed *Rails to Trails* magazine.

In this *Rail-Trail Hall of Fame* guidebook, discover two of the country's first rail-trails, Wisconsin's Elroy-Sparta State Trail and the Illinois Prairie Path; explore America's longest rail-trail, Katy Trail State Park, which spans Missouri; learn about the Chief Ladiga and Silver Comet Trails, which together form one of the longest paved pedestrian pathways in the nation; read about New York's famed High Line and stunning Hudson Valley Trail Network; and uncover many more national treasures.

These rail-trails represent pioneers of the movement; they inspired trail development across the nation, or they've revolutionized how trails can impact communities along their routes. Our Hall of Fame inductees are tangible realizations of our vision to create a more walkable, bikeable, and healthier America. No matter which route in this guidebook you decide to try, you're in for an unforgettable adventure.

What Is a Rail-Trail?

Rail-trails are multiuse public paths built along former railroad corridors. Most often flat or following a gentle grade, they are suited to walking, running, cycling, mountain biking, in-line skating, cross-country skiing, horseback riding, and wheelchair use. Since the 1960s, Americans have created more than 24,000 miles of rail-trails throughout the country.

These extremely popular recreation and transportation corridors traverse urban, suburban, and rural landscapes. Many preserve historical landmarks, while others serve as wildlife conservation corridors, linking isolated parks and establishing greenways in developed areas. Rail-trails also stimulate local economies by boosting tourism and promoting trailside businesses.

What Is a Rail-with-Trail?

A rail-with-trail is a public path that parallels a still-active rail line. Some run adjacent to high-speed, scheduled trains, often linking public transportation stations, while others follow tourist routes and slow-moving excursion trains. Many share an easement, separated from the rails by extensive fencing. At least 375 rails-with-trails exist in the United States.

What Is TrailNation™?

At RTC, we believe that communities are healthier and happier when trails are central to their design. Everything we love about trails gets better when we connect them, creating seamless trail networks that link neighborhoods, towns, cities, and entire regions together. That's why we're committed to connecting trails and building comprehensive trail systems that bring people together and get them where they want to go.

We've invested in eight TrailNation™ projects across the country—found in places that are diverse in their geography, culture, size, and scope—to prove what is possible when trail networks are central to our lives. One of those Trail-Nation projects can be found in the Washington, D.C., metropolitan region—the Capital Trails Coalition (CTC), which aims to create a vibrant model trail network anchored by the nation's capital and extending into surrounding Virginia and Maryland. You'll find the TrailNation project logo on the Washington & Old Dominion Railroad Regional Park entry of this book, as the rail-trail is a critical spine in the CTC. Learn more about RTC's vision to connect the country by trail at **trailnation.org**.

ABOUT THE CAPITAL TRAILS COALITION

The Capital Trails Coalition seeks to create an 800-mile network of multiuse trails that are equitably distributed throughout the Washington, D.C. metropolitan region, linking communities and major destinations, promoting physical activity, and spurring economic development and trail tourism. The regional trail network will transform public life by providing healthy, low-stress access to open space and reliable transportation for people of all ages and abilities. RTC is a founding partner in this coalition, which was conceptualized by the Washington Area Bicyclist Association. Learn more at **capitaltrailscoalition.org**.

What Is the Great American Rail-Trail™?

 A signature project of RTC, the Great American Rail-Trail is the organization's most ambitious trail project to date and will be the nation's first cross-country multiuse trail, uniting millions of people over its 3,700-plus-mile route between Washington, D.C., and Washington State. This unique journey through the District of Columbia and 12 states—Maryland, Pennsylvania, West Virginia, Ohio, Indiana, Illinois, Iowa, Nebraska, Wyoming, Montana, Idaho, and Washington—will make it possible for travelers to explore some of the country's most renowned geographic and cultural landmarks. Today, the Great American is more than 52% complete, but there are still more than 1,700 miles left to fill in. To get it done, RTC is providing the national leadership and on-the-ground support to bring together the people, plans, and partnerships necessary for completing the Great American Rail-Trail. Learn more at **greatamericanrailtrail.org.**

This scenic bridge over the Coeur d'Alene River is one of many along Idaho's Trail of the Coeur d'Alenes (see page 152).

How to Use This Book

Rail-Trail Hall of Fame provides the information you'll need to plan a rewarding rail-trail trek. With words to inspire you and maps to chart your path, it makes choosing the best route a breeze. Following are some of the highlights.

Maps

You'll find three levels of maps in this book: **an overall map of the country, regional locator maps,** and **detailed trail maps.**

Each chapter details a particular region's network of trails, marked on locator maps in the chapter introduction. Use these maps to find the trails nearest you, or select several neighboring trails and plan a weekend hiking or biking excursion. Once you find a trail on a regional locator map, simply flip to that trail's detail page for a full description. Accompanying trail maps mark each route's access roads, trailheads, parking areas, restrooms, and other defining features.

Key to Map Icons

| parking | drinking water | restrooms | featured trail | connecting trail | active railroad |

Trail Descriptions

Trails are listed in alphabetical order within each chapter. Each description leads off with a set of summary information, including trail endpoints and mileage, a roughness index, the trail surface, and possible uses.

The map and summary information list the trail endpoints (either a city, street, or more specific location) with suggested points from which to start and finish. Additional access points are marked on the maps and mentioned in the trail descriptions. The maps and descriptions also highlight available amenities, including parking and restrooms, as well as such area attractions as museums, parks, and stadiums. Trail length is listed in miles.

Each trail bears a **roughness index** rating from 1 to 3. A rating of 1 indicates a smooth, level surface that is accessible to users of all ages and abilities. A 2 rating means the surface may be loose and/or uneven and could pose a problem for road bikes and wheelchairs. A 3 rating suggests a rough surface that is recommended only for mountain bikers and hikers. Surfaces can range from asphalt or concrete to ballast, boardwalk, cinder, crushed stone, gravel, grass, dirt, sand, and/or wood chips. Where relevant, trail descriptions address alternating surface conditions.

5

All trails are open to pedestrians, and most allow bicycles, except where noted in the trail summary or description. The summary also indicates wheelchair access. Other possible uses include in-line skating, mountain biking, hiking, horseback riding, fishing, and cross-country skiing. While most trails are off-limits to motor vehicles, some local trail organizations do allow all-terrain vehicles (ATVs) and snowmobiles.

Trail descriptions themselves suggest an ideal itinerary for each route, including the best parking areas and access points, where to begin, your direction of travel, and any highlights along the way. Following each description are directions to the recommended trailheads.

Each trail description also lists a local website for further information. Be sure to visit these websites in advance for updates and current conditions. **TrailLink.com** is another great resource for updated content on the trails in this guidebook.

Trail Use

Rail-trails are popular destinations for a range of users, often making them busy places to enjoy the outdoors. Following basic trail etiquette and safety guidelines will make your experience more pleasant.

➤ **Keep to the right,** except when passing.

➤ **Pass on the left,** and give a clear, audible warning: "Passing on your left."

➤ **Be aware** of other trail users, particularly around corners and blind spots, and be especially careful when entering a trail, changing direction, or passing, so that you don't collide with traffic.

➤ **Respect wildlife** and public and private property; leave no trace and take out litter.

➤ **Control your speed,** especially near pedestrians, playgrounds, and heavily congested areas.

➤ **Travel single file.** Cyclists and pedestrians should ride or walk single file in congested areas or areas with reduced visibility.

➤ **Cross carefully** at intersections; always look both ways and yield to through traffic. Pedestrians have the right-of-way.

➤ **Keep one ear open and volume low** on portable listening devices to increase your awareness of your surroundings.

➤ **Wear a helmet** and other safety gear if you're cycling or in-line skating.

➤ **Consider visibility.** Wear reflective clothing, use bicycle lights, or bring flashlights or helmet-mounted lights for tunnel passages or twilight excursions.

➤ **Keep moving,** and don't block the trail. When taking a rest, turn off the trail to the right. Groups should avoid congregating on or blocking the trails. If you have an accident on the trail, move to the right as soon as possible.

➤ **Bicyclists yield** to all other trail users. Pedestrians yield to horses. If in doubt, yield to all other trail users.

➤ **Dogs are permitted** on most trails, but some trails through parks, wildlife refuges, or other sensitive areas may not allow pets; it's best to check the trail website before your visit. If pets are permitted, keep your dog on a short leash and under your control at all times. Remove dog waste in a designated trash receptacle.

➤ **Teach your children** these trail essentials, and be especially diligent to keep them out of faster-moving trail traffic.

➤ **Be prepared,** especially on long-distance rural trails. Bring water, snacks, maps, a light source, matches, and other equipment you may need. Because some areas may not have good reception for mobile phones, know where you're going, and tell someone else your plan.

Key to Trail Use

walking cycling wheelchair access in-line skating mountain biking

fishing horseback riding cross-country skiing snowmobiling

Learn More

To learn about additional rail-trails in your area or beyond, visit Rails-to-Trails Conservancy's trail-finder website, **TrailLink.com,** a free resource with more than 36,000 miles of mapped rail-trails and multiuse trails nationwide.

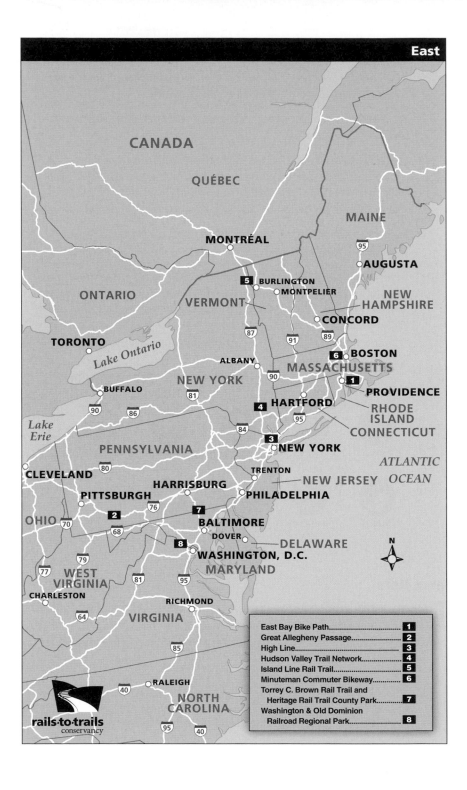

East

CANADA

QUÉBEC

MAINE

MONTRÉAL

AUGUSTA

BURLINGTON
MONTPELIER

ONTARIO

VERMONT

NEW HAMPSHIRE

CONCORD

TORONTO

Lake Ontario

ALBANY

BOSTON

MASSACHUSETTS

NEW YORK

BUFFALO

PROVIDENCE

HARTFORD

RHODE ISLAND

CONNECTICUT

Lake Erie

PENNSYLVANIA

NEW YORK

ATLANTIC OCEAN

CLEVELAND

TRENTON

NEW JERSEY

HARRISBURG

PITTSBURGH

PHILADELPHIA

OHIO

BALTIMORE

DOVER

DELAWARE

N

WASHINGTON, D.C.

WEST VIRGINIA

MARYLAND

CHARLESTON

RICHMOND

VIRGINIA

East Bay Bike Path................................. 1
Great Allegheny Passage....................... 2
High Line... 3
Hudson Valley Trail Network.................. 4
Island Line Rail Trail.............................. 5
Minuteman Commuter Bikeway.............. 6
Torrey C. Brown Rail Trail and
    Heritage Rail Trail County Park........... 7
Washington & Old Dominion
    Railroad Regional Park....................... 8

RALEIGH

NORTH CAROLINA

rails·to·trails
conservancy

EAST

The Western Maryland Scenic Railroad, which parallels a portion of the Great Allegheny Passage, offers tourism excursions (see page 14).

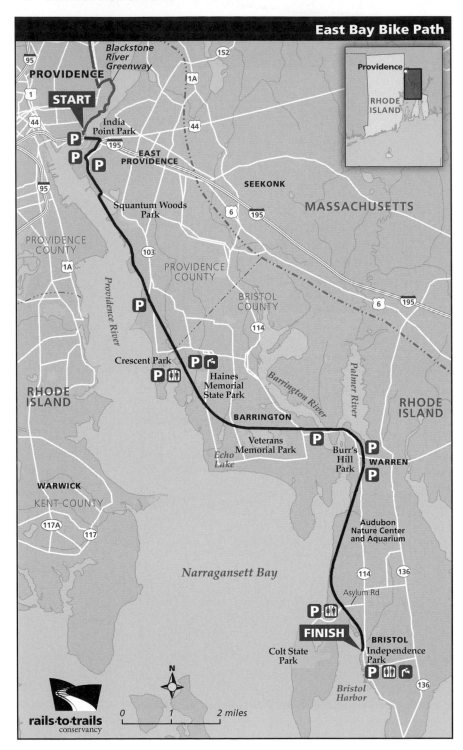

1 East Bay Bike Path

Featuring picturesque bay views replete with seabirds flying overhead and marinas full of ships displaying a panoply of colorful sails, the 14.3-mile East Bay Bike Path (EBBP) offers the quintessential New England experience. This was the first bike trail constructed by the state of Rhode Island, and since the first few miles opened in 1987, it has proven to be an immensely popular route for visitors and locals alike.

Begin in Providence at historical India Point Park. In the 1700s, this was a major port for trade ships traveling between the West Indies and east Asia. Later, the port was an entry point for waves of immigrants, including many Irish, Cape Verdeans, Azoreans, and Portuguese, whose impact on the culture of the region can still be felt today.

The waterfront pathway offers one beautiful scene after another.

Counties
Bristol, Providence

Endpoints
Tockwotton St. and India St. at India Point Park (Providence) to Thames St. and Oliver St. in Independence Park (Bristol)

Mileage
14.3

Roughness Index
1

Surface
Asphalt

The East Bay Bike Path has a distinct maritime flavor; you'll see marinas and boats of every size along the water.

Cross over the I-195 bridge and head south while enjoying stunning views of the Providence River. See tugboats and sailboats cruising along, spot swans and cormorants bobbing on the waves, and take in the fresh salty air on a leisurely ride along this well-maintained and well-used route.

In Riverside, take a detour to see the Looff carousel in Crescent Park. A National Historic Landmark, this hand-carved structure was built in 1895 by famed carousel maker Charles I. D. Looff, whose works were featured in amusement parks throughout the country. To reach the park, turn right onto Beach Road and take a left onto Bullocks Point Avenue.

As you continue along, the trail travels inland for a while, passing behind neighborhoods, wetlands, wooded areas, and parks, before skirting back along Narragansett Bay. Just south of Warren, look for an intersecting trail that will take you to the Audubon Nature Center and Aquarium (bike racks along the trail mark the spot). This state-of-the-art natural history museum and aquarium is the ideal place to acquaint yourself more fully with the marine environment of the region. Meander trails that wind through fresh and saltwater marshes, look inside a 33-foot life-size right whale, visit the center's rare blue lobster and orange lobster, and explore a number of interactive exhibits.

A little farther along, the trail ends at Independence Park near the Bristol Waterfront Historic District. Here you will find many shops and restaurants, as well as old buildings, churches, mills, and shipbuilding facilities that tell the history of this port town, which was founded in 1680.

RAIL-TRAIL HALL OF FAME SELECTION

With spectacular maritime views and an abundance of coastal wildlife, the EBBP offers a quintessential New England experience. Inducted into the Hall of Fame in 2009, the route is one of the most popular multiuse trails in Rhode Island.

RAILROAD HISTORY

Constructed in the mid-1800s, the corridor the EBBP follows was once the domain of one of New England's largest and most recognized railroads, the New York, New Haven & Hartford (the New Haven). The route carried freight and passengers before shutting down passenger service in 1937. Eventually the Penn Central Transportation Company took over the route due to a merger that subsumed The New Haven, but then the line was discontinued in 1973. In 1994 the R.I. Department of Transportation considered restoring the line for commuter service, but the value of the route as a multiuse trail and the expense of restoring the tracks curtailed this idea.

CONTACT: riparks.com/locations/locationeastbay.html

DIRECTIONS

To reach the Providence trailhead, take I-95 to Exit 19 and merge onto I-195 E. Take Exit 2 for India St. to Gano St. Turn left into India Point Park. The trailhead is on the right; ramps lead up to the bridge, where the path begins as a separated corridor alongside traffic.

There are many other places to park along the trail. The closest parking lots to the northern terminus are on Veterans Memorial Pkwy. in East Providence. Traveling east on I-195 from Providence, take Exit 4 to Riverside. In 0.3 mile, near Mercer St., you'll find two parking lots on the right.

To reach the Colt State Park trailhead in Bristol, take I-195 E into Massachusetts and take Exit 2. Follow MA 136 S 1.2 miles to Rhode Island, and continue on RI 136 S another 2.5 miles. Turn right onto Vernon St. in Warren, and then in 0.6 mile, turn left onto RI 114 S and go 2.3 miles toward Bristol. In Bristol, turn right onto Asylum Road and go 0.5 mile.

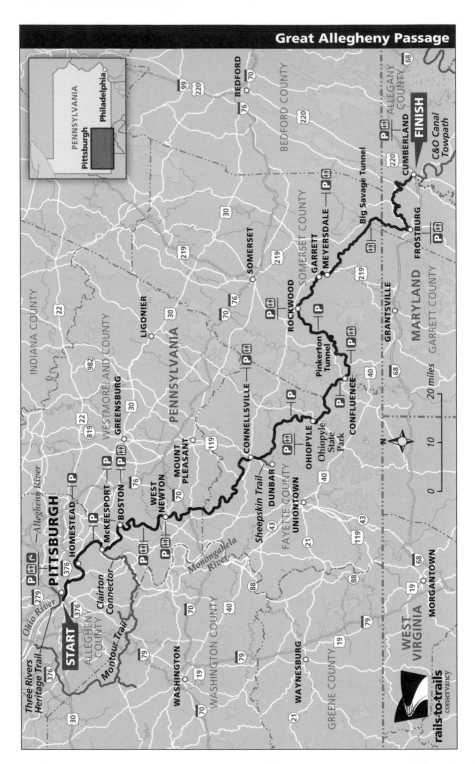

Great Allegheny Passage

Attracting thousands of visitors from across the country each year, the 150-mile Great Allegheny Passage (GAP) (**gaptrail.org**) is an ideal rail-trail for multiday exploration. The trail winds its way along scenic rivers and through dramatic mountain passes from Pittsburgh to Cumberland, Maryland, with numerous railroad relics and historical markers, as well as charming towns, lining the route.

The GAP is a host trail for the 3,700-plus-mile Great American Rail-Trail, which will one day form a seamless connection between Washington, D.C., and Washington State. It is also part of the September 11th National Memorial Trail that connects the World Trade Center, Flight 93, and Pentagon Memorials.

Begin at Point State Park in Pittsburgh. As you head south, you will cross the Monongahela River on a former railway bridge. Farther along, see remnants of the steel city's past in the form of a large industrial furnace, a ladle car, and a former steel mill, in addition to an array of interpretive signage.

The 150-mile trail offers countless stunning views.

Counties
MD: Allegany;
PA: Allegheny, Fayette,
Somerset, Westmoreland

Endpoints
Point State Park near
Commonwealth Pl. and
Liberty Ave. (Pittsburgh,
PA) to Chesapeake &
Ohio Canal National His-
torical Park at Canal St.
and Harrison St. (Cum-
berland, MD)

Mileage
150.0

Roughness Index
1

Surface
Asphalt,
Crushed Stone

The GAP's four tunnels, all located on the southern half of the trail, are well-loved features of the route.

All along the GAP, you experience a sense of remoteness and tranquility amid the beautiful landscape of lush forests, meadows of wildflowers, and sparkling rivers, but you're never too far from a town. The former industrial towns along the route that once were vital to the mining, steel, and glass industries now welcome trail users with a variety of amenities and services, the new mainstay to many of their economies. Follow the undulating Youghiogheny River and pass through several of these towns before reaching Ohiopyle. Here, find two dramatic trestles and some of the wildest rapids along the route. Popular with whitewater rafters, the river in this area features rocky outcrops, boulder-strewn banks, and soothing waterfalls.

Farther along, past the town of Confluence, where the Youghiogheny and the Casselman Rivers meet, the GAP heads northeast as it makes its way to the Eastern Continental Divide. Highlights of this section include traversing the restored 850-foot-long Pinkerton Tunnel; crossing the 100-foot-high Salisbury Viaduct, which spans more than 1,900 feet, and the slightly smaller Keystone Viaduct; and exploring the 3,300-foot-long Big Savage Tunnel, which offers welcome relief on hot summer days. (Note that this tunnel is closed late November–early April.) Along the way, enjoy spectacular views of the Casselman River Valley, which, in autumn, offers a vibrant display of colorful foliage.

Cross the Mason-Dixon Line and enter Maryland. In Frostburg, hop aboard the Western Maryland Scenic Railroad, a popular 3-hour steam locomotive excursion (open May–December), or continue your journey on the GAP for another 16 miles before reaching Cumberland. This is the end of the route, but it's the beginning of the Chesapeake & Ohio Canal Towpath, which ambitious cyclists can travel on for 185 miles to Washington, D.C.

RAIL-TRAIL HALL OF FAME SELECTION

In 2007 the GAP had the honor of being the first rail-trail inducted into the Hall of Fame. A destination trail that attracts visitors from throughout the country, the GAP offers a combination of beautiful natural surroundings on a well-maintained route that's rich in regional history and accommodating to multiday adventures.

RAILROAD HISTORY

The GAP follows the inactive lines of the Youghiogheny Branch of the Pittsburgh and Lake Erie Railroad (P&LE Yough Branch), which was built in 1883 and carried coal and coke to Pittsburgh, and the Western Maryland Railway (WM), which was built in 1912 and carried freight bound for Baltimore and points east. The two railways met in the town of Connellsville, about 60 miles south along the corridor, and were successful lines, until closing coal mines and the changing economies of the railroads forced the WM to close in 1975 and then the P&LE Yough Branch in 1991.

CONTACT: gaptrail.org

DIRECTIONS

To reach Point State Park at the northern end of the trail in Pittsburgh, Pennsylvania: From the east, follow I-376 W to Exit 70D/Stanwix St. Turn left at the light onto Fort Pitt Blvd. and bear right onto Commonwealth Pl. From the south and west, take I-79 N to Exit 59A for I-376. Take I-376 E 5.7 miles to Exit 70A/Boulevard of Allies, and turn right at the light onto Commonwealth Pl. From the north, take I-279 S to the Fort Duquesne Blvd. exit; almost immediately, turn right onto Stanwix St. Make the first right onto Penn Ave., and then bear right onto Liberty Ave. Turn right onto Commonwealth Pl. Parking is limited here, but garages are available within a short distance.

To reach the Cumberland trailhead in Maryland at the southern end of the trail: From I-68, take Exit 43B. Upon exiting, take a left onto W. Harrison St. and then an immediate right onto S. Mechanic St. The old Western Maryland train depot on your left has public parking for the trail.

Visit **atatrail.org** for more information about the many other access points along the Great Allegheny Passage.

High Line

NEW YORK
Albany

New York

Hudson River

Chelsea
Waterside Park

Pier 54

Hudson River Greenway

11th Ave

10th Ave

9A

9A

START

Whitney
Museum
of Art

Diller–
von Furstenberg
Sundeck

Chelsea
Market

Chelsea
Grasslands

Clement
Clarke
Moore Park

London
Terrace

MANHATTAN

NEW YORK COUNTY

Chelsea
Park

High Line
at the Rail Yards

FINISH

12th Ave

11th Ave

10th Ave

9th Ave

8th Ave

7th Ave

W 37th St
W 36th St
W 34th St
W 31st St
W 30th St
W 29th St
W 29th St
W 29th St
W 28th St
W 27th St
W 26th St
W 25th St
W 24th St
W 23rd St
W 23rd St
W 22nd St
W 21st St
W 20th St
W 19th St
W 18th St
W 17th St
W 16th St
W 15th St
W 14th St
W 13th St

Little West
12th St

Washington St

Gansevoort St

Hudson St

Horatio St

Jane St

Abingdon
Square

N

0   0.125   0.25 mile

rails·to·trails
conservancy

3 High Line

Towering 30 feet over 1.5 miles of Manhattan's West Side stands the spectacular High Line. Now a world-renowned tourist attraction and much-loved park, the High Line is constructed on a historical elevated freight rail line that for years stood unused. The structure had been an eyesore in the neighborhood, collecting trash and casting an ominous presence in an area that had seen better days. In 1999 two local residents banded together to save the structure from demolition, advocating for the line's preservation and reuse as a public space. Through much effort, their dreams were realized, exceeding everyone's expectations for what this space could be.

The High Line is not the first project of its kind in existence, but it is one of the most dynamic. As you stroll along the greenway, it is striking how the High Line offers

The elevated path is a recreation marvel that includes gardens and art.

County
New York

Endpoints
Gansevoort St. and Washington St. to W. 34th St. between 11th Ave. and 12th Ave. (New York City)

Mileage
1.5

Roughness Index
1

Surface
Concrete

a different experience throughout the corridor, with its varying design, surfaces that include concrete and bonded aggregate, a wide-open area of grass, and intimate contemplative pockets. At the southern entrance at Gansevoort Street, see views eastward to the Meatpacking District and westward to the Whitney Museum of American Art, as well as an abrupt cutoff where the elevated line had been severed in the 1990s. At the 14th Street Passage, a semienclosed space, see artwork presented by High Line Art. Farther along, take in river views as you lounge on chairs and sample from the seasonally operating food carts. Also take a detour and go back down to street level to wander through historical Chelsea Market, an ideal spot to pick up a gourmet lunch.

Throughout the route you will see a wide palette of plantings integrated into each section's unique design. With a nod to the corridor's neglected past, when plants grew wild among the inactive tracks, creating their own haunting beauty, the park features native self-seeding plants, such as coneflower, asters, sedges, goldenrods, and alumroot, laid out in an "intentionally unintentional" manner. Look closely and you'll find train tracks, and other relics of the railroad, peeking out from between plantings, a subtle but effective integration of past and present.

Portions of the High Line artfully incorporate characteristics of the former railroad corridor.

Wander the Chelsea Thicket, a narrow, winding, wooded pathway planted with roses; travel through a grove of big-leaf magnolias, sassafras, and service-berry at canopy level on the Falcone Flyover, a grated metal pathway; and explore a section where the concrete base has been removed to reveal the original structure of beams and girders (a favorite of children). After offering an expansive view of the Hudson River, the trail ends at 34th Street and 12th Avenue.

RAIL-TRAIL HALL OF FAME SELECTION

The High Line, a celebrated urban park and aerial greenway, joined the Hall of Fame in 2011. Incorporating cutting-edge landscape and architectural design into a historically significant structure that honors the former rail line, the park has been instrumental in the revitalization of the surrounding neighborhoods.

RAILROAD HISTORY

Beginning in the mid-1800s, street-level railroad tracks carried freight cars for the Hudson River Railroad along Manhattan's West Side. Due to numerous street crossings, blocks-long railcars, and general congestion, there were so many pedestrian fatalities that the route was nicknamed Death Avenue. In the 1930s a solution was found by elevating the track, eliminating 105 street crossings and allowing trains to load and unload directly inside buildings. Eventually, the rail line was supplanted by trucks, and the last train traveled on the High Line in 1980.

CONTACT: thehighline.org

DIRECTIONS

There are stairway access points at Gansevoort, 14th, 16th, 18th, 20th, 23rd, 26th, 28th, and 30th Sts., and 11th Ave. The route is wheelchair accessible, and elevators are available at Gansevoort, 14th, 16th, 23rd, and 30th Sts. **Bicycling on the High Line is prohibited;** however, you'll find racks to park your bicycle, or one of Citi Bike's, at street level in various locations.

The Gansevoort St. entrance at the southern end of the High Line can be reached via public transit, including the A, C, E, or L subway lines to W. 14th St. and Eighth Ave., or the 1, 2, or 3 lines to W. 14th St. and Seventh Ave. The 1 line can also be taken farther north to 18th St. or W. 23rd St. and Seventh Ave.; the C and E lines can also be taken farther north to W. 23rd St. and Eighth Ave. The M11 bus can be taken to Washington St., Ninth Ave., or 10th Ave. and W. 34th St.; the M14 bus can be taken to Ninth Ave.; the M23 or M34 buses can be taken to 10th Ave.; and the M12 bus can be taken to 12th Ave. and W. 33rd St.

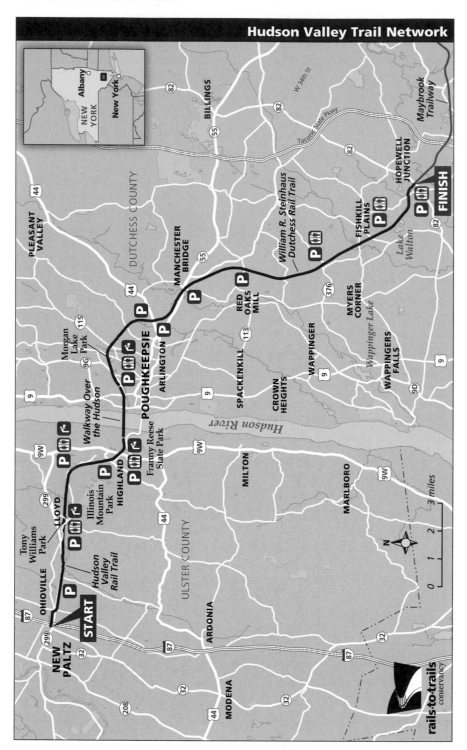

Hudson Valley Trail Network

Tucked into New York's picturesque Hudson Valley, a trio of connected rail-trails—the Hudson Valley Rail Trail, Walkway Over the Hudson, and William R. Steinhaus Dutchess Rail Trail—form a seamless paved pathway spanning nearly 22 miles. Together, they're also part of the Empire State Trail, a developing 750-mile trail network spanning the state from New York City to Canada and Buffalo to Albany.

Beginning on the west side of this trail trifecta, the Hudson Valley Rail Trail stretches 7.1 miles, connecting the towns of New Paltz, Lloyd, and Highland. From North Putt Corners Road in New Paltz, you'll head east, paralleling NY 299 through a mixture of commercial areas and wooded canopy. A highlight of this section is passage through Tony Williams Park, where you'll find athletic

A caboose from the early 20th century illustrates the history of the Hudson Valley Rail Trail.

Counties
Dutchess, Ulster

Endpoints
N. Putt Corners Road at NY 299/Main St. (New Paltz) to Martin Road and NY 82 (Hopewell Junction)

Mileage
21.8 combined (Hudson Valley Rail Trail: 7.1; Walkway Over the Hudson: 1.6; William R. Steinhaus Dutchess Rail Trail: 13.1)

Roughness Index
1

Surface
Asphalt, Concrete

The 212-foot-high bridge that comprises New York's Walkway Over the Hudson affords views in all directions.

facilities, picnic tables, and restrooms. Less than 0.5 mile from the park, the trail crosses over Black Creek, which is a popular waterway for kayakers and canoeists. Farther on, the trail runs along a rock cut, where you'll find wildflowers blooming in the crevices in the spring. The cut also provides a cool spot to relax on hot summer days.

Near the trail's midpoint, two magnificent arched bridges carry New Paltz Road over the corridor. Shortly thereafter, you'll reach the Highland Rotary Pavilion, named for the Highland Rotary Club, which has made the Hudson Valley Rail Trail a primary project for more than a decade. The park setting offers restrooms, a large parking lot, picnic tables, and drinking water.

Along the route, signage invites you to explore the history of the trail and the communities it connects, while trailside exercise stations encourage you to pause for a health and wellness moment. Approaching trail's end, you enter the hamlet of Highland and a more residential trail experience. A pedestrian bridge provides safe passage over US 44/NY 55/Vineyard Avenue as you continue through these more populated surroundings.

At its eastern end, the Hudson Valley Rail Trail meets the Walkway Over the Hudson State Historic Park, one of the longest pedestrian bridges in the world at 1.6 miles. The walkway opened in 2009 in commemoration of the 400th anniversary of Henry Hudson's historic 1609 journey up the river. From the bridge, the views of the Hudson River, 212 feet below, and its lush valley are simply breathtaking. Visitors are greeted by walkway volunteers and staff at welcome centers located at either end of the trail.

On its eastern end in Poughkeepsie, the Walkway Over the Hudson shares a parking lot with the William R. Steinhaus Dutchess Rail Trail, named for the county executive who championed it. The connecting trail continues 13.1 miles east through what seems like a perpetually green landscape of dense tree cover.

Traveling east from Poughkeepsie, the route passes a large golf course and Morgan Lake Park, a popular spot for fishing. After Morgan Lake, the trail begins to turn south, running through the communities of Arlington and LaGrangeville and skirting the eastern edge of Red Oaks Mill. This section includes an expansive bridge over NY 55, and the entire length of the trail features a mix of new bridges and converted railroad bridges and tunnels.

In Wappinger, trail users travel along a section called Veterans Memorial Mile, which features signage honoring each of the five branches of the military. Traversing a wooded corridor, this segment offers a quiet place to reflect and remember those who have served their country.

The path continues through the town of East Fishkill and ends in Hopewell Junction. At the terminus, you'll see the Hopewell Depot. Built in 1873, this former railroad station offers a museum and historical photo gallery inside. Across from the depot, visitors will also find a replica switching tower.

From here, future travelers will be able to connect to another rail-trail, the Maybrook Trailway, which will head to Brewster; the new trail is anticipated to open in fall 2020.

RAIL-TRAIL HALL OF FAME SELECTION

When the Walkway Over the Hudson's predecessor first opened in 1889, the railroad bridge was hailed as the Great Connector, as it offered a vital link between New England cities and supplies from Pennsylvania, the Midwest, and farther afield. Today, the bridge serves as a linchpin in a nearly 22-mile expanse of connected pathway. Two phenomenal rail-trails join the walkway and spin out into the communities on either side of the Hudson River: the Hudson Valley Rail Trail on the west bank and the William R. Steinhaus Dutchess Rail Trail to the east. Together, the three rail-trails were welcomed into the Rail-Trail Hall of Fame in 2016. They serve as a prime example of how integrated trail systems can produce important benefits for communities—for transportation, tourism, and economic development.

RAILROAD HISTORY

The Hudson Valley Rail Trail follows the former right-of-way of the New York, New Haven and Hartford Railroad. Two trailside cabooses, one dating to 1915

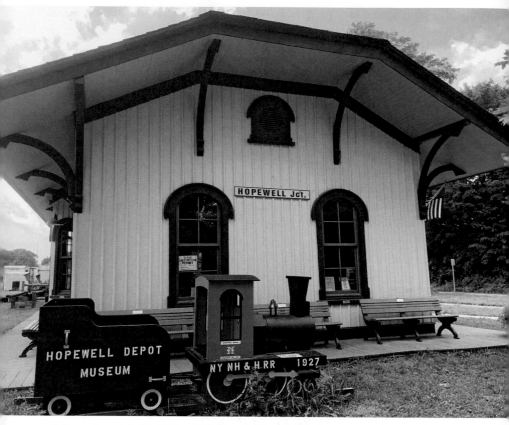

At the southern end of the William R. Steinhaus Dutchess Rail Trail is Hopewell Depot, built in 1873. Take time to explore the historical museum inside.

and the other to 1926, offer nods to the corridor's railroading past. The Walkway Over the Hudson was formerly the Poughkeepsie-Highland Railroad Bridge. The William R. Steinhaus Dutchess Rail Trail continues along what was once the Maybrook Line of the New York, New Haven and Hartford Railroad.

CONTACT: hudsonvalleyrailtrail.net, walkway.org, and
dutchessny.gov/Departments/Parks/Dutchess-Rail-Trail.htm

DIRECTIONS

Toward the west end of the Hudson Valley Rail Trail, ample parking is provided in Tony Williams Park in Lloyd. To reach the park from I-87, take Exit 18 for Poughkeepsie and New Paltz. Turn right onto NY 299 E, and go 2.3 miles. Turn right onto New Paltz Road, and go 0.7 mile. Turn left onto S. Riverside Road; after 0.1 mile turn right into the parking lot for Tony Williams Park.

On its east end, the Hudson Valley Rail Trail shares a trailhead with the Walkway Over the Hudson at 87 Haviland Road in Highland. To reach the parking lot in Highland from I-87, take Exit 18 for NY 299 E. Continue on NY 299 for 5 miles, then turn right onto US 9W S. Continue on US 9W for 2.1 miles, then turn left onto Haviland Road. Parking will appear on your left in 0.5 mile.

The Walkway Over the Hudson shares a trailhead with the William R. Steinhaus Dutchess Rail Trail at 61 Parker Ave. in Poughkeepsie. To reach the parking lot in Poughkeepsie from I-84, take Exit 13, and head north on US 9. Continue on US 9 N for 14.4 miles to NY 9G in Poughkeepsie; you will travel under the Walkway Over the Hudson on the way to this exit. Look for brown WALKWAY OVER THE HUDSON directional signs as you approach your exit. Turn right onto NY 9G, which becomes Washington St., and go 0.6 mile. Turn left onto Parker Ave. In 0.3 mile, a large parking lot will appear on your left.

Note: An ADA-compliant elevator, located in Poughkeepsie's Upper Landing Park (83 N. Water St.) near the Hudson River waterfront, goes up to the Walkway Over the Hudson bridge. However, the elevator operates seasonally and is weather dependent, so check the trail website before a visit.

To reach the trailhead parking lot in Hopewell Junction from I-84, take Exit 16N for the Taconic State Pkwy. Take the parkway 3.9 miles to Exit 41 for Beekman Road/County Road 9. Take a left onto Beekman Road, and continue 2.2 miles, when the road merges with NY 82. Take your next right after the merger; this will be Turner St. A parking lot will appear on your right almost immediately after the turn onto Turner St.

The trail system can also be reached by train; take an Amtrak train (**amtrak.com**) or Metro-North Railroad's Hudson Line (**mta.info/mnr**) from Grand Central Station in Manhattan to Poughkeepsie. The Poughkeepsie Station (41 Main St.) is 0.7 mile from the Walkway Over the Hudson entrance at Washington St.

Island Line Rail Trail

The Island Line Rail Trail (ILRT) follows the Lake Champlain shoreline north from Burlington, Vermont, with beautiful vistas of New York's Adirondack Mountains off in the distance. A distinctive feature of the trail is a 3-mile marble slab causeway, which gives riders the sensation of literally skimming the surface of Lake Champlain. The ILRT also travels over the Winooski River Bridge and includes a ride on a bike ferry.

Heading north from Oakledge Park in Burlington, travel along the shoreline of Lake Champlain before jutting inland for a short stretch and reaching the downtown area. This section of the trail is typically very busy, as it is popular with tourists as well as locals and is close to shops and restaurants. Continue along through Waterfront Park, which includes a boardwalk, boat launches, and a festival site that hosts various events during the year. As you head out of town, reach North Beach at mile marker 3.4 and Leddy Park at mile marker 5.1, both of which offer parking and amenities.

Skirting the Lake Champlain shoreline, the path offers beautiful views overlooking the water.

Counties
Chittenden, Grand Isle

Endpoints
Austin Dr. in Oakledge Park between Dunder Road and Ambrose Pl. (Burlington) to Martin Road between Railroad St. and South St. (South Hero)

Mileage
13.4

Roughness Index
1

Surface
Asphalt, Gravel

One of the special features of the ILRT is the Winooski River Bridge. The bridge is structurally quite striking with a 2,500-foot elevated boardwalk that takes bikers and pedestrians over the environmentally sensitive Colchester Delta Park floodplain. But the truly unique aspect of the trail is the Colchester Causeway. Biking along the marble causeway gives riders the thrilling sensation of riding over water. Even the most seasoned biker will enjoy this unusual feature. Along the way, you'll see American elms lining the path. The trees lean sharply from the harsh lake winds, yet have found a refuge here from elm disease that has infected much of their species. As you ride along, look for warblers and kingfishers, common birds for the area. Note that the last few miles of the ILRT are unpaved and not well suited for road bikes.

The causeway is abruptly interrupted in Lake Champlain at "The Cut," a small gap. Here you can board a bike ferry for a short shuttle over the gap to continue another 1.5 miles to the trail's end in the town of South Hero.

RAIL-TRAIL HALL OF FAME SELECTION

The ILRT offers the opportunity to bike through one of New England's most vibrant towns, take in dramatic lakefront views with a stunning mountain backdrop, and enjoy a variety of unique experiences, from traversing bridges to gliding over the lake on a causeway and traveling on a bike ferry. It is no wonder that the trail joined the Hall of Fame in 2010.

RAILROAD HISTORY

The rail corridor that the ILRT follows was created in 1899 by the Rutland-Canadian Railroad to connect the New England coast with the Great Lakes. In addition to laying track, the railroad built 6 miles of marble causeways and trestles to span Lake Champlain. For more than 60 years, the railway operated along this route, carrying passengers and freight, especially dairy and other agricultural products. At its peak, with its considerable network, the railroad stretched for more than 400 miles across upstate New York and through Vermont.

Congress's railbanking act of 1968, which allowed disused rail corridors to be preserved for future use through interim conversion to trails, helped support the development of thousands of miles of trails but also received challenges by opponents. In a 1996 decision for the case *Preseault v. United States,* which concerned a tract of land in Burlington, Vermont, the Supreme Court unanimously ruled in favor of the constitutionality of railbanking. The land became the Burlington Bike Path, which is now the Island Line Rail Trail.

The Lake Champlain causeway offers a unique trail experience.

CONTACT: localmotion.org

DIRECTIONS

To reach the Oakledge Park trailhead at the southern end of the trail in Burlington, take I-89 N to Exit 13 and follow I-189 W 1.4 miles to US 7. Turn right onto US 7 N, and in 0.5 mile turn left onto Flynn Ave. Follow Flynn 1 mile to its end, and look for signs to Oakledge Park. There are plenty of parking and amenities here. This trailhead is wheelchair accessible and connects to the portion of the trail that is paved.

To reach the northernmost trailhead: From US 2 in South Hero, take South St. 2.5 miles to Martin Road; turn right and continue 0.3 mile to the parking area on the left.

Additional trailheads with parking and amenities include North Beach, Leddy Park, and Airport Park, and trail access is easy throughout the downtown area.

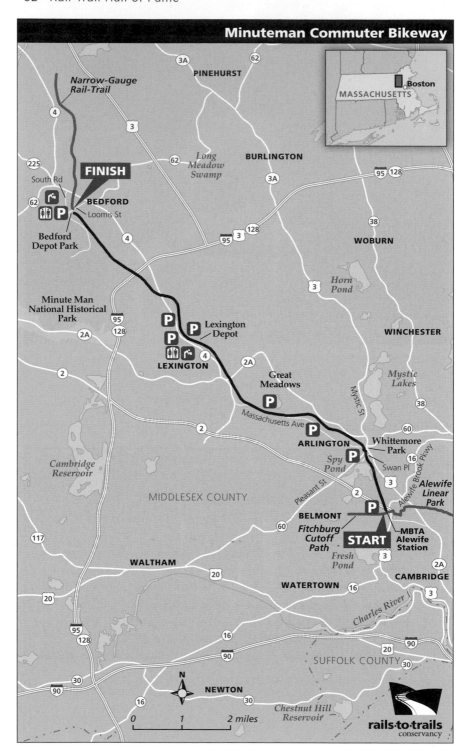

Minuteman Commuter Bikeway

Boston

MASSACHUSETTS

Narrow-Gauge
Rail-Trail

PINEHURST

Long
Meadow
Swamp

BURLINGTON

FINISH

BEDFORD

South Rd

Loomis St

Bedford
Depot Park

Minute Man
National Historical
Park

WOBURN

Horn
Pond

Lexington
Depot

LEXINGTON

WINCHESTER

Great
Meadows

Mystic
Lakes

Massachusetts Ave

Mystic St

ARLINGTON

Whittemore
Park

Cambridge
Reservoir

Spy
Pond

Swan Pl

Alewife
Brook Pkwy

Alewife
Linear
Park

MIDDLESEX COUNTY

Pleasant St

BELMONT

*Fitchburg
Cutoff
Path*

START

MBTA
Alewife
Station

WALTHAM

Fresh
Pond

CAMBRIDGE

WATERTOWN

Charles River

SUFFOLK COUNTY

N

NEWTON

Chestnut Hill
Reservoir

0   1   2 miles

rails·to·trails
conservancy

6 Minuteman Commuter Bikeway

Named after the patriotic colonists who would be ready at a minute's notice to face off against the British during the American Revolutionary War, the 10.1-mile Minuteman Commuter Bikeway travels through the towns where these men lived and fought. Located just outside of Boston, the trail travels from West Cambridge through the famous Revolutionary towns of Arlington and Lexington, before ending in Bedford. Rich in history, the trail also serves the community by connecting to schools, neighborhoods, shops, restaurants, and public transportation.

The Minuteman Commuter Bikeway is a wonderful resource, but visitors should be aware that on warm weekends, this trail can be difficult to navigate due to the throngs of people it attracts. This is not a reason to avoid it, but do plan ahead and try to avoid peak times.

Parts of the bikeway run through a wooded corridor.

County
Middlesex

Endpoints
MBTA Alewife Station at Alewife Station Access Road at Concord Turnpike/MA 2 (Cambridge) to Bedford Depot Park at South Road and Loomis St. (Bedford)

Mileage
10.1

Roughness Index
1

Surface
Asphalt

The trail is popular year-round.

The trail begins right outside the MBTA Alewife station in West Cambridge and heads north to Arlington. At mile marker 1.5, the route can get confusing, as it appears to abruptly end at Swan Place. Turn right and then take a quick left onto Massachusetts Avenue (ride either on the road or sidewalk along this busy street). Turn right at the intersection with Pleasant Street, cross over to the north side, and look for the trail behind the Uncle Sam Memorial Statue (Cyrus E. Dallin Art Museum and Whittemore Park will be across the street on your right).

In Lexington, stop at The Lexington Depot to learn more about the town's role in the Revolutionary War. Built in 1847, the restored depot now serves as the headquarters for the Lexington Historical Society. Also visit the trailside visitor center to see a diorama of the Battle of Lexington, and wander the Battle Green, located just across the street. It was here on April 19, 1775, that 77 Minutemen faced off in the first skirmish with the British. See the oldest war memorial in the country, completed in 1799, honoring the eight patriots who lost their lives in this conflict.

The trail ends at Bedford Depot Park, where you will find amenities and information about the area. For rail enthusiasts, the park also features a restored railroad depot and the Freight House, both listed on the National Register of Historic Places, as well as a beautifully restored Budd Rail Diesel Car. Here you can learn more about the railroad history of the Minuteman Commuter Bikeway, obtain information about the area, or just relax from your ride.

RAIL-TRAIL HALL OF FAME SELECTION

From events that took place along the route during the American Revolutionary War to the economic lifeblood it provided as a rail line and its present-day use connecting towns in a car-free transportation corridor, the Minuteman Commuter Bikeway is an incredible community resource. This rail-trail joined the Hall of Fame in 2008.

RAILROAD HISTORY

In 1846 the Boston & Maine Railroad's Lexington Branch was established between West Cambridge and Lexington (an extension to Bedford and Concord was built in 1873). The route was an important economic link for the agricultural towns to the commercial hub of Boston. At its peak, two dozen passenger and two local freight trains operated along the route. By 1958 service had declined, and the Massachusetts Bay Transportation Authority (MBTA) took over the commuter-rail route. Eventually, service was discontinued, and the corridor became a trail in 1992.

CONTACT: minutemanbikeway.org

DIRECTIONS

To reach the West Cambridge trailhead by car, take I-95 to Exit 29A and head east on the Concord Turnpike/MA 2 toward Arlington and Cambridge. At the end of the turnpike, bear right onto Alewife Brook Pkwy. and turn right onto Cambridge Park Dr. to the MBTA Alewife station. Park in the adjacent garage. The trail begins near the northwest corner of the station and heads north.

To access the trailhead via the T, take the Red Line to the northern end (Alewife station). Bikes are allowed on the Red Line during off-peak hours (they are not allowed on all lines, however, so check in advance if transferring).

To reach the Bedford trailhead, take I-95 to Exit 31B and head north toward Bedford on MA 4/225. Drive 2 miles and turn left onto Loomis St. The trailhead is at the South Road intersection at the Bedford Depot Park in 0.4 mile.

Trailhead access is also available in Arlington and Lexington.

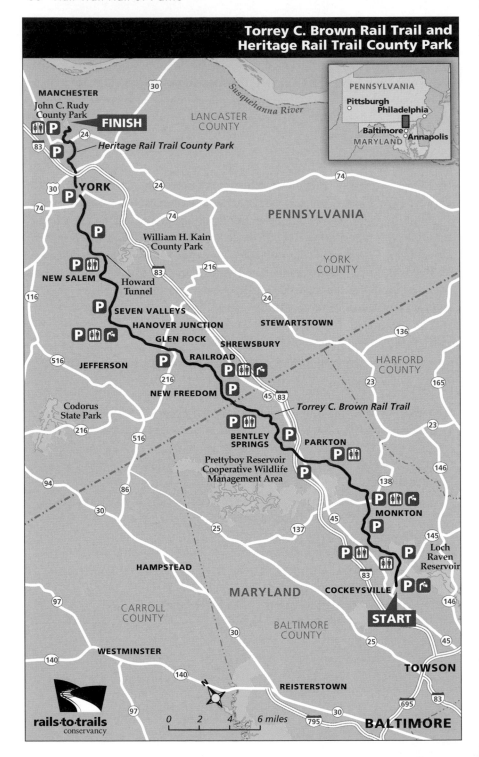

Torrey C. Brown Rail Trail and Heritage Rail Trail County Park

7 Torrey C. Brown Rail Trail and Heritage Rail Trail County Park

Cross the Mason-Dixon Line and experience a bit of history along the Torrey C. Brown Rail Trail (TCB) and Heritage Rail Trail County Park (HRT). Combined, the trails cover nearly 47 miles and stretch from just outside of Baltimore north to York, Pennsylvania. Visitors should plan to spend plenty of time exploring the several museums and sites along the way that detail this region's fascinating place in Civil War and railroad history.

Previously known as the Northern Central Railroad Trail, the TCB is one of the oldest rail-trails in the country, and it travels nearly 20 miles on a flat crushed-stone surface. Beginning in Cockeysville, Maryland, travel through several small towns, including Monkton, home to the beautifully restored 1898 Monkton Train Station that now houses a small railway museum. Also pass historical towns, such as Parkton and Bentley Springs. Along the way look for other traces of the route's railroad past in the form of whistle posts, mileage markers, and position light signals. In New Freedom, Pennsylvania, the trail

Counties
Baltimore (MD),
York (PA)

Endpoints
Ashland Road near Clay Hill Cir. (Cockeysville, MD) to John C. Rudy County Park at Mundis Race and Dellinger Roads (York, PA); the two trails meet at the Maryland–Pennsylvania state line near Orwig Road in New Freedom, PA

Mileage
46.9 combined
(TCB: 19.5; HRT: 27.4)

Roughness Index
1

Surface
Asphalt, Crushed Stone

Steam Into History tourist trains are a welcome attraction along the trail.

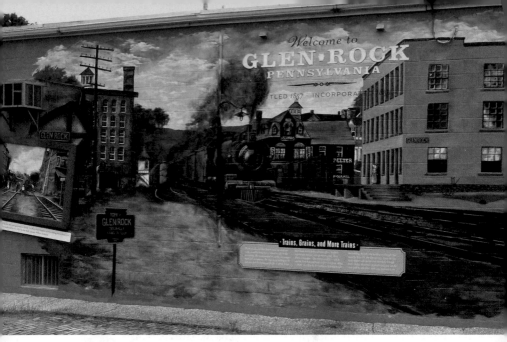

Enjoy this trailside mural in the Pennsylvania community of Glen Rock.

makes a seamless transition to the 27.4-mile HRT. Here, find the New Freedom Train Station, restored to its 1940s appearance. The station now houses a railroad museum and includes an actual-size K-4 engine diorama, original working freight scale, and original safe.

Travel through farmlands and along the banks of Codorus Creek before arriving in Hanover Junction. During the Civil War, the station here was a telegraph office and served as the major source of communications between Gettysburg and Washington, D.C. During the Battle of Gettysburg, at least 10,000 troops passed through, and President Abraham Lincoln changed trains in Hanover Junction on his way to deliver the famed Gettysburg Address. Later, Lincoln's body was transported through here en route to burial in Springfield, Illinois. Now visitors can learn more about these and other events related to the Civil War at the station's museum, which has been restored to its 1863 appearance.

Between New Freedom and Hanover Junction, history buffs can also experience a connection to the past on the Steam Into History excursion train that parallels the trail. The train is pulled by a replica 1860s locomotive, and costumed historical figures and musicians frequently perform on board.

Leaving Hanover Junction, head 5 miles north to the 370-foot-long Howard Tunnel in Seven Valleys. Built in 1838, the stone-arch tunnel is one of the oldest in the country. Following Codorus Creek, the HRT continues north to York. In 5 miles, you'll cross the city's Grantley Road. From here through the remainder of the trail northward, horses are not permitted.

The beautifully wooded Torrey C. Brown Rail Trail is part of Gunpowder Falls State Park.

Continue another mile to North Pershing Avenue and West Philadelphia Street, where a temporary, signed, on-road connection begins. The connection navigates approximately six blocks within the City of York before connecting back to the trail at the intersection of North George Street and Hamilton Avenue. Plans are in the works to move this segment off road by fall 2020.

The trail continues along the west side of Codorus Creek until it reaches US 30, where it then crosses over the creek via a pedestrian walkway that leads to a trail parking lot at Loucks Mill Road and US 30. The path passes underneath US 30 and then heads north 4.5 miles, ending at York's 150-acre John C. Rudy County Park, which has parking, restrooms, sports fields, pavilions, a dog park, and a variety of other outdoor amenities.

RAIL-TRAIL HALL OF FAME SELECTION

The TCB and HRT, which joined the Hall of Fame together in 2015, offer an exciting journey through both railroad and Civil War history. The combined routes feature an impressive number of remnants from the railroad, and the excellent trailside museums tell of the region's role in American history.

RAILROAD HISTORY

Connecting Baltimore and Harrisburg, the Northern Central Railway once traveled the corridor now used by the TCB and HRT. Built in the 1830s, the route

Much of the route of this rail-trail pair offers a serene, natural experience.

was in operation until a section was washed out by Hurricane Agnes in 1972. During the Civil War, the railway was used to supply Northern troops heading south and, during the Gettysburg campaign, the lines were often a target, with several bridges north of York destroyed.

CONTACT: dnr.maryland.gov/publiclands/Pages/central/tcb.aspx and yorkcountytrails.org/trails/heritage-rail-trail-county-park

DIRECTIONS

To reach the southern trailhead: Follow I-83 N and take Exit 20A to merge with Shawan Road toward Cockeysville, Maryland. After a mile, turn right onto York Road, and then in 0.3 mile turn left onto Ashland Road. Bear right to stay on Ashland and follow it 0.6 mile to the end, where the trailhead can be found. Parking is not available here but may be found on nearby streets.

To reach the trailhead at the Maryland–Pennsylvania border (New Freedom, Pennsylvania), from I-83, take Exit 4 toward Shrewsbury, and then turn east onto PA 851/E. Forrest Ave. After 0.7 mile, turn left onto S. Main St. Go 1.1 miles, and turn right onto Constitution Ave. After 1.9 miles, turn left onto E. High St., and go 0.3 mile. Turn right onto Singer Road. Take Singer Road 0.4 mile, and take the third left (0.4 mile) onto Orwig Road. The trailhead is 0.5 mile ahead on your right.

To reach the trailhead in downtown York, Pennsylvania: From I-83, take Exit 22 (N. George St.). Follow N. George St. south about 2 miles and turn right onto W. Philadelphia St. Go two blocks and turn right onto Pershing Ave. Park on the street.

Numerous access points and parking areas are along the route. Refer to the websites above for more details.

8 Washington & Old Dominion Railroad Regional Park

The Washington, D.C., area has many fantastic rail-trails, but the Washington & Old Dominion Railroad Regional Park (W&OD) stands out as one of the best. Traveling 45 miles from just outside the city into the rolling hills of Virginia's Piedmont, the route offers a tranquil respite, connecting several towns and providing a recreational haven.

The W&OD begins in Arlington, Virginia, running parallel to a strip of industrial and commercial buildings. While this may not be a grand start, take comfort in knowing that this short stretch is the least attractive of the route and that the scenery will quickly improve. Cross Columbia Pike and enter into a heavily wooded area, which immediately changes the tone of the route. Near the East Falls Church Metro, the trail goes on-road for a couple of blocks

The trail traverses the leafy suburbs of Northern Virginia.

Counties
Arlington, Fairfax, Loudon

Endpoints
S. Four Mile Run Dr. and Shirlington Road (Arlington) to 21st St./ VA 690 near N. 23rd St. (Purcellville)

Mileage
45.0

Roughness Index
1

Surface
Asphalt, Concrete

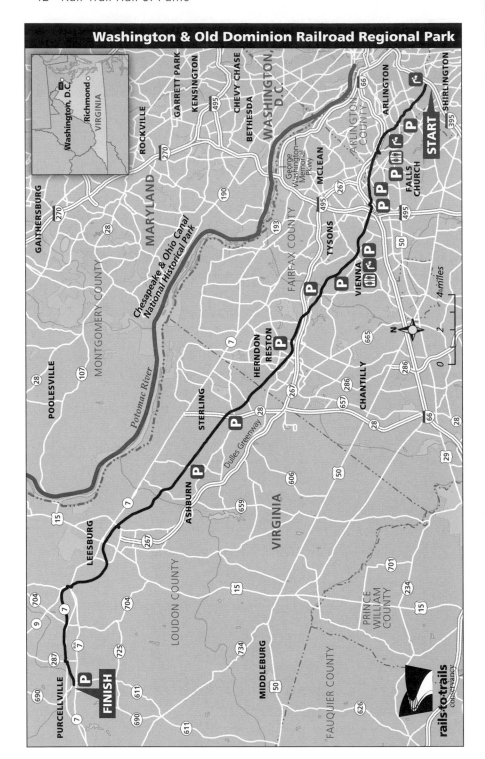

The trail ends at the Purcellville Train Depot, which dates back to 1904 and provides amenities for trail users.

and, while there is signage, it is not well marked. In Benjamin Banneker Park (where you will see a baseball field), take the first right onto a small path, bear right at the end, and follow North Tuckahoe Street for two blocks until you pick the trail back up again.

As you continue along, the trail winds through the back of several neighborhoods along a wooded corridor before entering the town of Vienna and later Herndon. Both towns offer water fountains, a bike shop, and a variety of restaurants (restrooms are available trailside in Vienna). The W&OD is a popular trail and, on weekends in particular, you won't be lonely. But, as you head farther outside Washington, D.C., the crowds thin out. In Ashburn, stop to see a working quarry that is located right along the trail and provides an interesting rest stop.

In historic Leesburg, wander the charming downtown and grab a bite at one of the numerous restaurants (turn right onto King Street and head two blocks to reach downtown).

The W&OD does have some hills, and as you travel farther west, you will encounter these more frequently. But you will also find some of the most striking scenery here, as you pass through rolling farmland dotted with grazing horses and cows and wooded areas that provide shade on a hot day. After Leesburg, amenities are nonexistent along the trail until you reach the end in Purcellville. This charming town, which has a number of Victorian-era buildings, offers a bike shop and restaurants, including a trailside spot popular with W&OD riders.

The west end of the trail offers picturesque scenery through rolling farmland and charming rural communities.

RAIL-TRAIL HALL OF FAME SELECTION

From its urban beginning to its end in pastoral farm country, the W&OD covers a lot of ground and provides both an ideal recreational corridor and a popular pathway for bike commuters. This exemplary rail-trail also serves as an important spine in the Capital Trails Coalition's developing 800-mile network of multi-use trails in the Washington, D.C. metropolitan region. The trail joined the Hall of Fame in 2008.

RAILROAD HISTORY

The W&OD takes its name from the railroad that ran through the corridor from 1859 to 1968. The route was built with the intention of bringing coal from the Appalachians to the port of Alexandria, but tracks were never laid past the Blue Ridge Mountains, and then what did exist was severely damaged during the Civil War. The railway's most successful run was in the early 20th century when passenger service was offered three times a day to towns along the route. Mismanagement, the growth of the trucking industry, and an increase in private car ownership ultimately caused the railway's demise.

CONTACT: wodfriends.org or nvrpa.org/park/w_od_railroad

DIRECTIONS

To begin at the southern end of the W&OD Trail, from I-395 N, take Exit 6 (Shirlington). Exit right onto S. Shirlington Road. In 0.2 mile, at the second traffic light, arrive at S. Four Mile Run Dr. The W&OD Trail parallels the road. You can park along the side of the road, but it is not advisable to leave your car overnight here. In fact, you're better off parking in one of the parking garages just across the road in downtown Shirlington.

To begin at the northern end in Purcellville, from Arlington, take I-66 W to Exit 67 (VA 267). Follow VA 267 for 2.7 miles to Exit 16 (VA 7). Follow VA 7 W 30.6 miles. Exit at VA 287 and turn left. Follow VA 287 for 0.7 mile, and turn right onto VA 7 Business. After 1.3 miles, turn right again onto 23rd St., which becomes 21st St. The Purcellville Train Depot is 0.25 mile away on the right. Parking is across the street, but there are time limits during certain days of the week. Unlimited parking time is permitted at a small lot one block east along the trail off Hatcher Ave.

Parking and trail access are available in dozens of places along the route; see **wod friends.org.**

Cardinal Greenway............ **9**
Elroy-Sparta State Trail...... **10**
George S. Mickelson Trail.... **11**
Illinois Prairie Path.......... **12**
Katy Trail State Park......... **13**
Little Miami Scenic Trail...... **14**
Midtown Greenway........... **15**
Monon Trail................. **16**
Paul Bunyan State Trail....... **17**
Pere Marquette Rail-Trail...... **18**
Prairie Spirit Trail State Park... **19**
Wabash Nature Trail.......... **20**

CANADA

NEW YORK

PENNSYLVANIA

HARRISBURG

CLEVELAND

WEST VIRGINIA

VIRGINIA

CHARLESTON

RICHMOND

NORTH CAROLINA

Lake Erie

OHIO

COLUMBUS

CINCINNATI

FRANKFORT

KENTUCKY

TENNESSEE

MICHIGAN

DETROIT

LANSING

Lake Superior

Lake Michigan

INDIANA

INDIANAPOLIS

MADISON

MILWAUKEE

CHICAGO

ILLINOIS

SPRINGFIELD

ST. LOUIS

JEFFERSON CITY

MISSOURI

WISCONSIN

SAINT PAUL

MINNEAPOLIS

IOWA

DES MOINES

KANSAS CITY

TOPEKA

MINNESOTA

NORTH DAKOTA

BISMARCK

SOUTH DAKOTA

PIERRE

RAPID CITY

FARGO

NEBRASKA

OMAHA

LINCOLN

KANSAS

OKLAHOMA

COLORADO

DENVER

N

rails-to-trails
conservancy

MIDWEST

Indiana's Monon Trail has several distinctive bridges that add to its charm (see page 77).

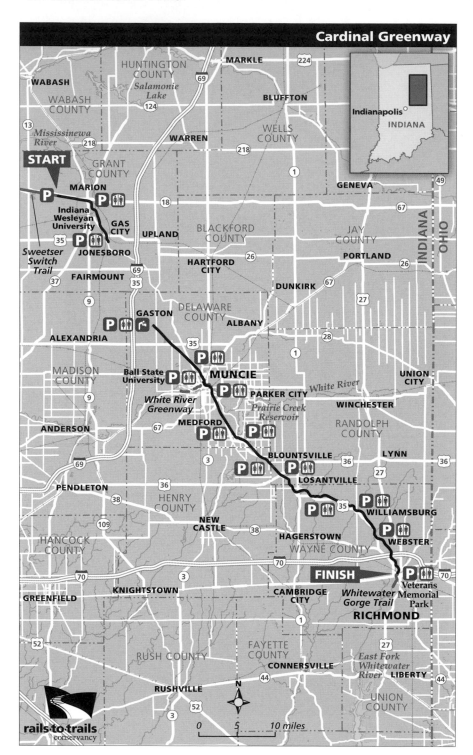

The Cardinal Greenway, the longest rail-trail in Indiana and a 2018 inductee into the Rail-Trail Hall of Fame, stretches over 61 miles from Marion to Richmond along a former CSX railroad corridor. The trail takes its name from the *Cardinal*, the passenger train that once regularly ran the route.

The long greenway connects Marion, Muncie, Losantville, Richmond, and other smaller towns in rural Indiana. The Cardinal Greenway is also a host trail for the 3,700-plus-mile Great American Rail-Trail, which will one day form a seamless connection between Washington, D.C., and Washington State. The well-maintained trail is open sunrise–sunset and is mostly flat for its entire length. The design elements along the path are consistent throughout, with arched steel embellishments on bridge crossings and stone mile markers every 0.5 mile.

Look for wildflowers along the Cardinal Greenway in the spring and summer.

Counties
Grant, Delaware, Henry, Randolph, Wayne

Endpoints
County Road 400 W just south of IN 18 (Marion) to E. 10th St. just east of Boyd St. (Jonesboro); W. CR 850 N, 0.1 mile west of Broad St. (Gaston), to the intersection of N. Third St. and N. D St. (Richmond)

Mileage
61.2

Roughness Index
1

Surface
Asphalt

Scenic farm landscapes with rustic barns and silos dot the southern section of the Cardinal Greenway.

Starting just north of Marion, the Cardinal Greenway connects to the Sweetser Switch Trail, which heads north, while the Cardinal Greenway runs south. For a brief stretch at the northernmost section of the Cardinal Greenway, the path runs adjacent to and then crosses over an active Norfolk Southern line, as the trail travels toward the heart of Marion through a flat, rural landscape that highlights industrial and farmland scenery.

Heading southeast into Marion, you will pass by the Miller Avenue trailhead with informational kiosks and ample parking. From there, you'll cross over the first of nine bridges along the trail and pass through Hogin Park in the center of Marion.

On the southeast end of Marion, the trail winds through a beautifully wooded section, crossing over Deer Creek before arriving at US 35 on the north side of the village of Jonesboro. The Jonesboro trailhead lies just south of the US 35 intersection on the east side of the trail. A slight uphill climb takes you to a bridge that overlooks the Mississinewa River.

An 11.3-mile gap in the Cardinal Greenway currently exists from Jonesboro to Gaston due to private landowners acquiring the former rail corridor. An on-road route has been designated between the two towns and can be found on the official trail website, **cardinalgreenways.org.**

Wildflowers flank the Gaston section of the greenway during the spring and summer. As you reach the County Road 400 trailhead on the north side of Muncie, the urban fingers of the town start to reach out. An influx of runners, walkers, and in-line skaters—many of them students at nearby Ball State University—hit the trail.

In the heart of Muncie is the beautifully restored Wysor Street Depot, which is listed on the National Register of Historic Places and serves as the main office of Cardinal Greenways, Inc. Farther south at IN 32, the new Kitselman trailhead—named after the brothers who, more than a century ago, built the nearby Indiana Steel & Wire Company factory—allows for a connection to Muncie's 5.6-mile White River Greenway, which follows the trail's eponymous river, stretching from the west side of Muncie to the John M. Craddock Wetland Nature Preserve.

At the Kitselman trailhead, you will also be faced with two bridges: to the right, a historical trestle bridge; to the left, the bicycle and pedestrian bridge that takes you across the White River.

While traveling south you'll pass through Muncie's quiet residential neighborhoods until you reach Mansfield Park on the left, which unofficially marks the end of the Muncie section of the trail. Passing under US 35, you will reenter the sun-drenched Indiana countryside, where the trail meanders along the highway through Medford, where equestrians can access the 3.5-mile Cardinal Greenway Horse Trail that parallels the paved Cardinal Greenway and extends to CR 534 East. The Medford trailhead features a circular gravel lot with hitching posts and room for horse trailers.

The newest section of the Cardinal Greenway runs from Losantville south to Richmond, continually changing from open, sunny stretches to shady sections under a wooded tree canopy. From Losantville to Williamsburg, much of the trail runs adjacent to the road, but your eye is instead drawn to scenic wood bridges and farmlands, with rustic barns and silos around every corner. This stretch of the route has light traffic, giving it a remote feeling, and is relatively flat with a slight downhill grade. From Williamsburg to Richmond, the path shows its rail roots with a stretch on an elevated railbed. As you pass through Webster, the trail begins a slight uphill grade through woodlands; this is a good spot for birding.

As the greenway approaches the outskirts of Richmond, you will pass under I-70 and through local parks and woodlands. The trail is no longer elevated as it makes its way through residential areas.

Along the final mile of the Cardinal Greenway, the trail features a trestle bridge over the East Fork Whitewater River before its official end at the D Street trailhead. From the trailhead, the greenway connects to the 3.5-mile Whitewater Gorge Trail, which heads southwest to Test Road. The Whitewater Gorge Trail features geological landmarks, such as vertical cliffs and waterfalls, which are accessible via side paths.

RAIL-TRAIL HALL OF FAME SELECTION

Rails-to-Trails Conservancy was pleased to announce the Cardinal Greenway as the 2018 Rail-Trail Hall of Fame inductee, chosen through a national vote held in the summer. The longest rail-trail in Indiana, the Cardinal Greenway has served as a local economic asset for more than 25 years—made possible by strong

community leadership and volunteerism and by connecting the region's picturesque rural landscapes, suburban communities, and urban centers.

RAILROAD HISTORY

Constructed at the turn of the 20th century, the Cincinnati, Richmond and
Muncie Railroad (CR&M)—later purchased by the Chesapeake & Ohio Railway
(C&O)—shuttled passengers, coal, merchandise, and other goods from Cincinnati to Chicago, with stops in its three namesake cities. Passenger service on
the CR&M line declined steadily through the 1940s, ending in 1949. The C&O
would eventually integrate with the Baltimore & Ohio Railroad in 1963, starting a series of mergers and acquisitions that ultimately led to the formation of
CSX. The CR&M line ceased to operate in 1986, and freight service rerouted
through Indianapolis. Efforts to transform the disused line into the Cardinal
Greenway—named for the last passenger train in regular service on the route—
began some 7 years later as a volunteer effort.

CONTACT: cardinalgreenways.org

DIRECTIONS

To access the northernmost trailhead just north of Marion: From I-69, take Exit 264 for IN 18.
Head west on IN 18, and go 10.8 miles. Turn left onto County Road 400 W. The trailhead and
parking lot for the Sweetser Switch Trail (which serves both the Sweetser Switch Trail and the
Cardinal Greenway) will be on your right. Cross the railroad tracks to access the Cardinal Greenway on the east side of CR 400 W.

To reach the trailhead in Gaston, take I-69 to Exit 255 for IN 26 toward Hartford City.
Head east on IN 26, and go 1.5 miles. Turn right onto S. Wheeling Pike, go 3 miles, and turn
right onto S. CR 900 E, which becomes N. CR 600 W. In 4.9 miles, turn right onto CR 850 N/W.
Elm St. In 0.3 mile, turn left onto Broad St. The trailhead is 0.1 mile straight ahead, on the west
side of the parking lot.

To access the southernmost trailhead near Veterans Memorial Park in Richmond: From
I-70, take Exit 149 or 149A, and head south on Williamsburg Pike. In 2.4 miles, turn left onto
Richmond Ave. In 0.6 mile, cross the East Fork Whitewater River, and Richmond Ave. becomes
N. D St. Go 0.1 mile after crossing the river, and turn right onto N. Fifth St. Take an immediate
right onto N. D St. The parking lot is 0.1 mile straight ahead. The trailhead is on your right, just
under the Richmond Ave. Bridge.

Set amid a classic Wisconsin landscape of rolling hills, farmlands, and pastures dotted with grazing cows, the 33.8-mile Elroy-Sparta State Trail (EST) offers a fun and relaxing recreational corridor. But what makes the route truly special are three dramatic railroad tunnels that burrow deep through rock, plunging trail users into almost pitch darkness.

The trail's hard-packed crushed limestone base is comfortable for walking and running, and it's suitable for most bicycle tires. It's a popular route, and in the five small towns along the way, you'll find many businesses that cater to trail users. Take advantage of shuttle services that are provided by several vendors in order to travel one-way along the trail; enjoy bike-friendly inns; and

Because of the harsh winters, each tunnel was fitted with large doors that are still in place today.

Counties
Juneau, Monroe

Endpoints
WI 82 at WI 71 (Elroy) to S. Water St. and Milwaukee St./La Crosse River State Trail (Sparta)

Mileage
33.8

Roughness Index
1

Surface
Crushed Stone

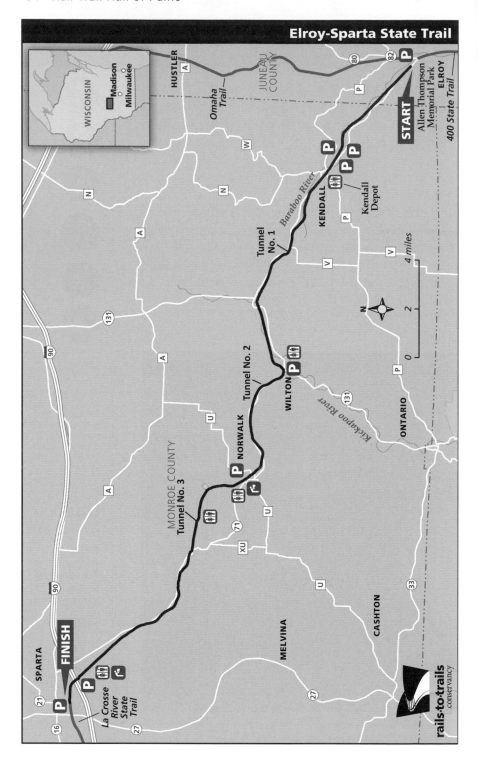

Elroy-Sparta State Trail

The old Norwalk Creamery was operational in the early 1900s.

find trailside restaurants. Note that all Wisconsin rail-trails require users to purchase a day-use permit. These are available at trailheads and other locations in the area.

Begin in Elroy and travel west toward Sparta. In Kendall, stop at the trail headquarters in the restored Kendall Depot, which also houses a railroad history museum complete with photos, railroad artifacts, and a large history mural. A little more than 3 miles along, reach the first of the three tunnels. Both this tunnel and the second (which is located between the towns of Wilton and Norwalk) run 0.25 mile straight through rock, with only a pinprick of light visible at the other end. The third tunnel lies about 3 miles past Norwalk and is considered to be the most dramatic of the three. It's about 0.75 mile long, resulting in a completely dark passage. Bicyclists should walk their bikes through the tunnels and be sure to bring a flashlight!

You will notice heavy wooden doors at the entrance and exit of each of the tunnels. During the time of the railroad, the tunnels were manned by watchmen, who would open and close them for each passing train during winter months to avoid snow accumulating inside. The doors are still used today, blocking entrance November–May.

In addition to offering an exciting and unique trail experience, the EST also connects to other rail-trails that are part of a network spanning more than 100 continuous miles from the Mississippi River through the heart of Wisconsin farm country, allowing for days of exploration. In Elroy, link to the 22-mile 400 State Trail and, in Sparta, find the 21-mile La Crosse River State Trail.

RAIL-TRAIL HALL OF FAME SELECTION

The Elroy-Sparta State Trail, established by the Wisconsin Department of Natural Resources in 1965 and opened to the public in 1967, was a pioneer of the rail-trail movement. In 2008 it joined the Hall of Fame. The iconic tunnels, links to the state's network of rail-trails, and classic Wisconsin scenery make this a well-loved and memorable adventure for all trail users.

RAILROAD HISTORY

The Chicago & North Western Railway's main line once traveled the route of the Elroy-Sparta State Trail. Connecting Chicago with the Twin Cities of Minnesota and North and South Dakota, the railroad was an important route that supplied Midwestern cities with goods from agricultural centers, including cattle that were carried to the Chicago stockyards. At its height, 6 passenger trains and up to 50 freight trains passed through this corridor each day. The route was established in 1873, but by the early 20th century a more efficient bypass was created. The line was lightly used for decades afterward, before use of it was finally discontinued in the mid-1960s.

CONTACT: dnr.wi.gov/topic/parks/name/elroysparta

DIRECTIONS

To reach the Sparta trailhead: From I-90, take Exit 25 to head north on S. Black River St. Take the first right onto Avon Road. In 0.6 mile, the road will split; veer left onto S. Water St. In 0.3 mile, turn right onto Milwaukee St., and look for the parking lot and trailhead immediately on your right at the Sparta Area Chamber of Commerce (111 Milwaukee St.).

To reach the Elroy trailhead: From I-90/I-94, take Exit 69 to WI 82 W/Gateway Ave. in Mauston. Go west on WI 82 for 12 miles to Elroy; turn left onto WI 71/Main St. when the roads intersect downtown. In 0.4 mile, look for the parking lot on your right in Allen Thompson Memorial Park.

Additional parking lots and restrooms are available in the other towns the trail crosses: Norwalk, Wilton, and Kendall.

11 George S. Mickelson Trail

Experience a piece of Wild West history along the 109-mile George S. Mickelson Trail (GMT) as it travels from the former gold-mining boomtown of Deadwood south over old railroad bridges, through rock tunnels, and into the heart of the Black Hills. Named after the late South Dakota governor who was instrumental in getting the trail built, this spectacular rail-trail delivers an unparalleled opportunity to immerse yourself in a stunning landscape while reliving a bit of the Old West.

Founded illegally in the 1870s on land that had been granted to the Lakota, Deadwood once epitomized a lawless frontier town. At the trailhead, stop by the railroad history museum, located in a restored engine house, to learn more about the town (the building also houses a bike shop). Note that a permit is required to use the GMT. This

The trail winds through a variety of beautiful landscapes, such as this high mountain meadow near Mystic.

Counties
Custer, Fall River, Lawrence, Pennington

Endpoints
US 85 near Cedar Lane at the old railroad depot (Deadwood) to E St. near SD 471 (Edgemont)

Mileage
109.0

Roughness Index
2

Surface
Crushed Stone

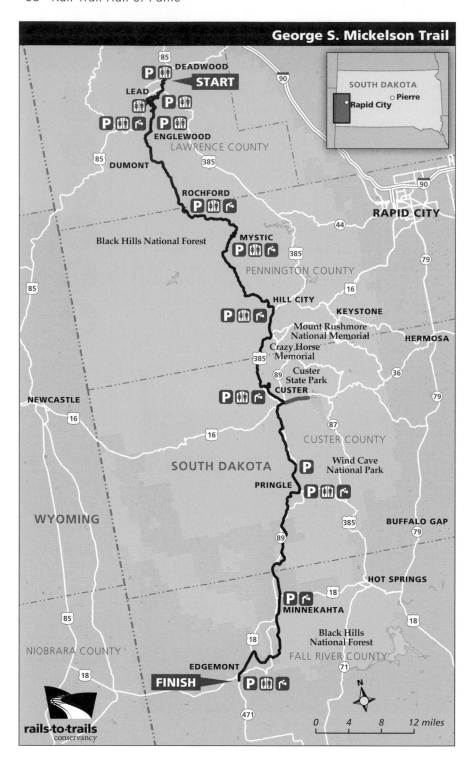

The path is a popular tourist destination in all seasons.

can be purchased ($4 per day) at self-pay stations located at trailheads. Several vendors offer shuttle services along the route. See the website on page 60 for information about fees, shuttles, and more.

Head south from Deadwood to take advantage of the downhill, which includes sections with a 4 percent grade. The GMT winds its way through a variety of landscapes, from dense forests of ponderosa pine, through narrow valleys, to high mountain meadows and open prairie. Reach the highest point, at just over 5,700 feet, north of the town of Dumont. Pass through historical mining towns such as Lead and Englewood, visit the ghost towns of Rochford and Mystic, and at mile marker 49.6 (markers start at the southern end) take in a beautiful view of the Crazy Horse Memorial. All along the route, see remnants from the railroad, travel more than 100 converted railway bridges, traverse four dramatic tunnels that burrow through rock, see an old caboose in Custer, and spot pieces of railroad bed in several locations.

Wildlife abounds in the Black Hills. Keep alert for bighorn sheep, mountain goats, elk, jackrabbits, and pronghorn antelope, as well as the occasional cattle that may wander into your path on sections that are along private property. In Custer, take a 3-mile spur to Custer State Park, which is home to bison, coyotes, and prairie dogs. Pass through a couple more former mining towns, as well as the town of Minnekahta, which in the 1890s attracted tourists to its hot springs. Continue another 16 miles to Edgemont, where the trail ends next to an operational railroad.

RAIL-TRAIL HALL OF FAME SELECTION

Completed in 1998, the George S. Mickelson Trail is an exceptional recreational route that offers fascinating Wild West folklore; is rich in railroad, mining, and American Indian history; and travels through some of the most spectacular landscapes in the country. It was inducted into the Hall of Fame in 2010.

RAILROAD HISTORY

Once gold was discovered in the region in 1874, numerous towns and railroads sprang up in the Black Hills, seemingly overnight. While sections of the GMT were established earlier, in the 1890s the route from Deadwood to Edgemont was built by the Grand Island & Wyoming Central Railroad and became known as the High Line. This line became part of the Chicago & North Western in 1903 and remained successful until the Great Depression. Passenger service was eliminated in 1949, but a portion of the route remained operational until as late as 1986.

CONTACT: gfp.sd.gov/parks/detail/george-s--mickelson-trail

DIRECTIONS

There are 15 trailheads along the route. To reach the Deadwood trailhead and parking lot: Take I-90 to Exit 17 (US 85). Follow US 85 S for 8.7 miles toward Deadwood. Turn left onto Deadwood St. and take an immediate right onto Sherman St.; in town, the road becomes Charles St. In 0.3 mile look for the red historical CB&Q Engine House with a large parking lot on your right (just before the Cedar Lane intersection); this is the trailhead.

To reach the trailhead in Edgemont: From Rapid City, take SD 79 S for 51.9 miles. Turn right onto US 18 and follow it 5 miles into Hot Springs. Turn left to continue on US 18 another 24.1 miles. Turn left onto 10th Ave. and then make an immediate left onto SD 471, heading south to downtown Edgemont. Follow the highway 0.6 mile to Second Ave., and turn right. Go 0.3 mile to E St., and turn left. Continue until the street ends at the railroad tracks; an unpaved parking lot will be on your right.

The Illinois Prairie Path (IPP) began as the vision of one woman, naturalist May Theilgaard Watts. In 1963 the *Chicago Tribune* published her letter to the editor describing the potential for an unused railway right-of-way to become a footpath lined with native plants. Her vision became the vision of numerous volunteers who worked to make this dream a reality. Covering 58 miles and traveling from Chicago into the western suburbs, the route includes a main branch and four spurs that each link up with different sections of the Fox River Trail.

The hub for the IPP is in Wheaton at the corner of West Liberty Drive and South Carlton Avenue. Stretching eastward, the **Main Branch** is a 16-mile urban route that begins on city streets and heads east along West Liberty Drive (distinct green markers guide the way). Once on

The path provides year-round outdoor adventure.

Counties
Cook, DuPage, Kane

Endpoints
Forest Park Transit Center at Van Buren St. and Des Plaines Ave. (Forest Park) to W. Liberty Dr. and S. Carlton Ave. (Wheaton), where spurs lead to Aurora, Batavia, Geneva, and Elgin, all ending at points along Fox River Trail

Mileage
58.4

Roughness Index
1–2

Surface
Asphalt, Concrete, Crushed Stone

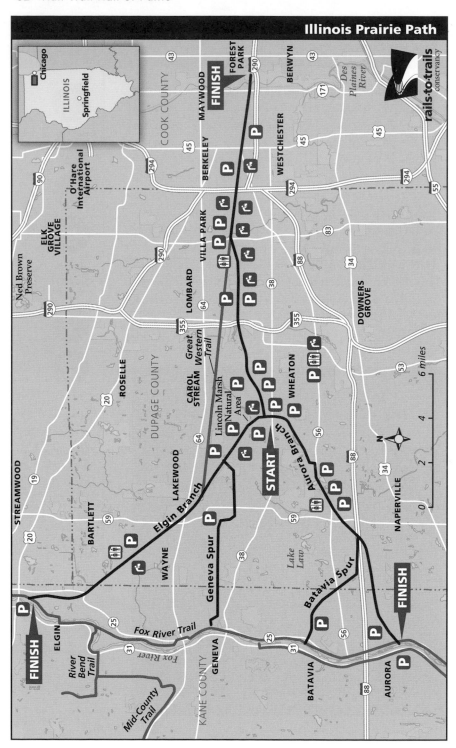

Parts of the trail have a quiet, wooded feel.

the trail, spend the first 2 miles enjoying a rail-with-trail experience, as the IPP shares the corridor with a commuter line. In Villa Park, stop to see the historical displays at the restored train depot. This branch of the IPP ends at the Forest Park Chicago Transit Authority Station.

Back at the Wheaton hub, head south on South Carlton Avenue, again following IPP markers, before reaching the off-road portion of the 13-mile **Aurora Branch.** After leaving Wheaton behind, the route becomes tranquil, passing through woodlands and fields. Just before the trail crosses I-88, look for the **Batavia Spur** on the right. This 6-mile spur travels along a forested path to the town of Batavia. Back on the Aurora Branch, the trail surface becomes asphalt before reaching its endpoint at the Fox River.

At the IPP hub back in Wheaton, head north on the 14-mile **Elgin Branch.** This branch begins off-road and, after crossing over streets and an active rail line, enters the bucolic Lincoln Marsh Natural Area. Continue along and turn left at Geneva Road to reach the 9-mile-long **Geneva Spur,** which travels through the upscale suburb of Geneva. Farther along on the Elgin Branch, intersect with the 12-mile-long Great Western Trail (which meets up with the IPP once again in Villa Park along the Main Branch). For the remainder of the route, enjoy a rural landscape of fields and wooded areas before ending in Elgin.

RAIL-TRAIL HALL OF FAME SELECTION

The IPP is the result of the hard work of volunteers who recognized the potential for the unsightly and unused right-of-way that passed through their communities. The rail-trail, one of the first such trails in the country, joined the Hall of Fame in 2008. The route offers a visually appealing corridor for both commuters and recreational trail users, linking towns and connecting to other rail-trails on its multibranched network.

RAILROAD HISTORY

The IPP follows almost the entire right-of-way of the former Chicago, Aurora & Elgin Railroad. Known as the Roarin' Elgin or Great Third Rail, this electric commuter railroad provided service from the western suburbs to downtown Chicago. The railroad was built to very high standards, could reach speeds of 65 miles per hour, and was predominantly double-tracked. The IPP operated from the late 19th century to 1957, when it so abruptly shut down service that passengers were stranded (freight service continued for a while afterward). The route's decline came from the increase in private car ownership and the completion of the Eisenhower Expressway in 1955.

CONTACT: ipp.org

DIRECTIONS

Trailhead access is available at many points along the route.

To reach the hub in Wheaton: From I-355 take Exit 24 to IL 38/Roosevelt Road. Travel west 2.2 miles and turn right onto Lorraine Road. After 0.7 mile, turn left onto Hill Ave., and in 0.3 mile turn right onto Prospect Ave. Continue north on Prospect about 300 feet until the road dead-ends in a parking lot for Hoffman Park. In the northeast corner of the parking lot, you'll see a paved trail that leads to the Illinois Prairie Path.

To reach the Forest Park Transit Center (711 Des Plaines Ave.) trailhead by train, take the Chicago Transit Authority (CTA) Blue Line to the end. The CTA system connects Chicago and its surrounding suburbs. Bikes are allowed on the train during off-peak hours. The station does have limited parking (for a $6 daily fee) and is easily accessible off I-290, if driving. From I-290 E, take Exit 21A for Des Plaines Ave.; turn left onto Des Plaines Ave., and in 0.1 mile you will turn left into the station.

Traversing almost the entire state of Missouri, the nearly 240-mile Katy Trail State Park (the Katy) is the longest rail-trail in the country. The corridor follows an inactive rail line, which now attracts thousands of people who come to experience the beauty of the region along a well-maintained recreational route rich in history. Traveling parallel to the majestic Missouri River for a large section, with limestone bluffs to one side and the river to the other, the trail features some of the most striking natural areas of the state, as it winds through dense forests, wetlands, valleys, prairies, and rolling hills, in addition to weaving through more than 40 towns.

The Katy begins northwest of St. Louis in Machens and heads westward alongside the Missouri River, passing through the state capital in Jefferson City and, via a spur,

Tourists flock to the Katy Trail because of its status as the longest rail-trail in the country.

Counties
Boone, Callaway, Cole, Cooper, Henry, Howard, Montgomery, Pettis, St. Charles, Warren

Endpoints
Machens Road near MO 94 (Machens) to E. Sedalia Ave. near Price Lane (Clinton)

Mileage
239.6

Roughness Index
2

Surface
Crushed Stone, Gravel

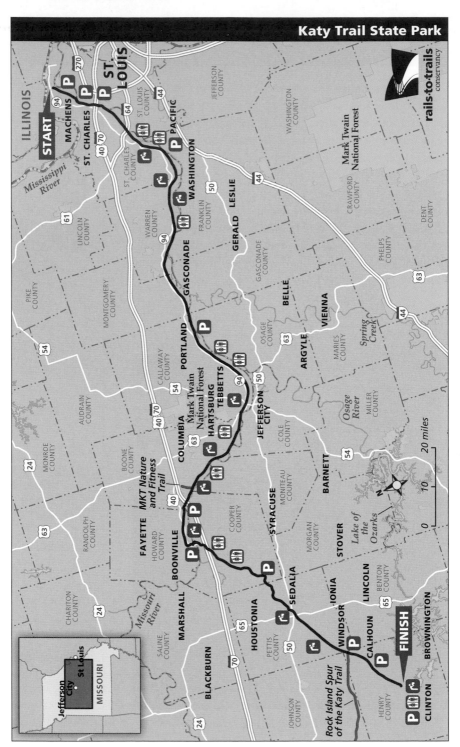

Former railroad bridges and other historical treasures dot the rail-trail.

Columbia. It then leaves the river behind, turning southwest to its endpoint in Clinton. The route is relatively flat and, although built for walkers and cyclists, does allow horseback riding in the western section from the state fairgrounds in Sedalia to Calhoun, and in the midwestern section from Portland to Tebbetts. Frequent washouts were a challenge when the railway was operating along this route. This is still true today, and, before setting out, all trail users should check with the Missouri Department of Natural Resources, which maintains the trail, to learn of any sections that may be closed.

As you travel the Katy, enjoy the amenities of the numerous small towns, many of which had been reliant on the railroad and have seen their economies revitalized since the rail-trail was created. Today, many inns, restaurants, and businesses cater to trail users, and, for intrepid souls seeking to bike the entire route, it is easy to find inns and bike shops that will provide shuttle services, making the logistics that much simpler. MO 94, known as Missouri's wine road for the number of wineries (and breweries) located along it, also runs close to the Katy for almost 100 miles, with many vineyards easily accessible from the trail.

Between St. Charles and Boonville, the Katy has been designated an official segment of the Lewis and Clark National Historic Trail, and the entire route is part of the American Discovery Trail, as well as a Millennium Legacy Trail. Both at trailside markers and in towns along the way, learn more about historical events that shaped this region, and see numerous relics from the former railroad.

At Windsor, travelers can connect to the Rock Island Spur of Katy Trail State Park, which stretches nearly 50 miles northwest to Pleasant Hill, a suburb of Kansas City. Eventually, more rail-trail will be developed through the Rock Island corridor, heading east from Windsor to connect with the Katy a second time near Washington. Together, the Katy Trail and the Rock Island Spur will form a continuous rail-trail loop and cover nearly 450 miles between Kansas City and St. Louis.

RAIL-TRAIL HALL OF FAME SELECTION

The Katy was the second trail added to the Hall of Fame in 2007, and its length alone makes it noteworthy. But the route's stunning natural beauty, importance to the dozens of communities it traverses, and well-preserved historical legacy are what truly make this rail-trail outstanding.

RAILROAD HISTORY

The Katy follows the route of the former Missouri-Kansas-Texas Railroad. Originally referred to as the K-T for its stock exchange symbol, it later evolved into the Katy. The railway ran from the late 1800s until 1986, when it ceased operations, but throughout its existence it was plagued with problems, including inefficient routing and flooding from the overflowing Missouri River.

CONTACT: mostateparks.com/park/katy-trail-state-park

DIRECTIONS

There are numerous trailheads along the route. The above website includes specific details, including wheelchair accessibility, for each of the trailheads.

Note that the eastern trailhead in Machens is not accessible by car, though you can pick up the trail at the nearby St. Charles trailhead. To reach it: From I-70, take Exit 229 for Fifth St. Once on S. Fifth St., head north 0.3 mile to the intersection with Boone's Lick Road; veer right onto Boone's Lick and follow it 0.5 mile to the large parking lot near the south end of Frontier Park.

To reach the western trailhead in Clinton: From I-49, take Exit 157 (MO 7). Follow MO 7 S for 37.8 miles to Clinton, and exit onto MO 52. At the end of the exit ramp, you'll see the parking lot next to a green caboose labeled MKT. (The trail itself continues slightly farther to E. Sedalia Ave., but parking isn't available there.)

inding its way from the outskirts of Cincinnati for 78 miles through state parks and small towns, the Little Miami Scenic Trail (LMST) is part of a vast network of paved off-road trails that travel throughout southwestern Ohio. The LMST alone offers a long, tranquil route through a scenic portion of the Buckeye State, but, combined with other trails with which it intersects, it also allows the potential for a multiday exploration of Ohio's Miami Valley.

The LMST is often thought of in terms of its southern and northern sections, with the dividing line being the town of Xenia. The southern section begins in Anderson Township, which lies east of downtown Cincinnati, on the eastern bank of the Little Miami River. From there, it's 3.2 miles to Newtown through an area that feels largely rural, despite its proximity to the city.

The Yellow Springs Bridge is one of many charming sights along the way.

Counties
Clark, Clermont, Greene, Hamilton, Warren

Endpoints
OH 32 and Beechmont Ave. (Anderson) to W. Jefferson and S. Center Sts. (Springfield)

Mileage
78.1

Roughness Index
1

Surface
Asphalt, Concrete

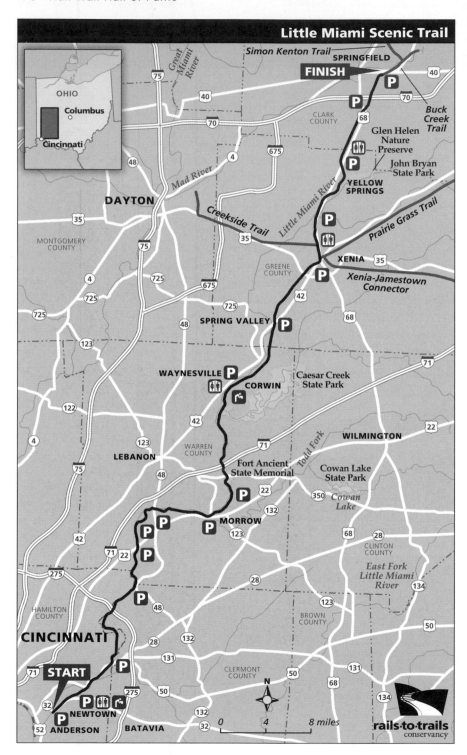

The Massie Creek Bridge between Yellow Springs and Xenia Station offers picturesque views.

Beyond Newtown, the trail runs alongside the Little Miami River for much of the way, traveling through quiet countryside, forests, and fields on a shaded route that passes through several small towns offering shops and restaurants. Along the way, see a former railway depot in Morrow, stop to visit the American Indian archaeological site of Fort Ancient, and cross an old iron trestle in Corwin.

Farther along, reach Xenia (where mileage markers start over at 0). The restored rail depot at Xenia Station is the hub of three other rail-trails—Creekside Trail, Xenia-Jamestown Connector, and Prairie Grass Trail—and the beginning of the northern portion of the LMST. Past Xenia, the LMST leaves the river behind and skirts alongside beautiful wooded areas, including Glen Helen Nature Preserve, which is across the street from Antioch College in Yellow Springs. Stop to wander this tranquil oasis or stroll the small downtown, which has a number of quirky shops and restaurants. In town, see reminders of the LMST's railroad past in the form of two converted train cabooses that serve as storefronts, as well as the Yellow Springs Railroad Station, which now houses the Chamber of Commerce.

It is about 7 miles, with a gradual uphill grade, to the trail's end in Springfield. Sections around Springfield can be confusing, as portions are on the road and involve street crossings, not all of which are well marked. Follow bike lanes that link off-road sections of the trail before ending at the Heritage Center of Clark County. From here, connect with the Simon Kenton Trail, which travels more than 35 miles north, and, slightly farther along, to the 6-mile Buck Creek Trail, which goes through town.

RAIL-TRAIL HALL OF FAME SELECTION

The Little Miami Scenic Trail, which joined the Hall of Fame in 2009, offers a long, uninterrupted route through a beautiful southwestern Ohio landscape and is immensely important to the communities through which it passes.

The rail-trail is also a significant component of both the 340-mile network of paved trails in Ohio's Miami River Valley region and the cross-state Ohio to Erie Trail, which spans more than 270 miles from the Ohio River in Cincinnati to Lake Erie in Cleveland.

RAILROAD HISTORY

In 1841 the first 15 miles of track for the Little Miami Railroad (LMRR) were laid from Cincinnati, with the entire route that the LMST currently follows open by 1845. The route was meant to spur economic development, as at that time the only transportation arteries in the area were waterways. Unfortunately, east-west routes operated by larger railroads proved more lucrative, and the LMRR never became more than a second-tier route. In the 1870s, it was acquired by the Pittsburgh, Cincinnati & St. Louis Railway, and, in the 1970s, by Conrail, who soon after discontinued the line.

CONTACT: miamivalleytrails.org/trails/little-miami-scenic-trail

DIRECTIONS

Trailheads are located throughout the route.

To reach the southern trailhead in Newtown: From I-275, take Exit 63 to OH 32 W/James A. Rhodes Appalachian Hwy. Follow OH 32 W for 4.1 miles, and turn right onto Round Bottom Road. In 0.4 mile turn left onto Valley Ave. Continue 0.5 mile until the road ends at the Little Miami Golf Center (3811 Newtown Road), where you will find the trailhead and parking.

To reach the trail hub about midway in Xenia: From Dayton, take US 35 E for 11.6 miles into Xenia. Continue straight on US 35 Bus./W. Main St. 2.7 miles. Turn right onto S. Church St., which turns right and becomes Cincinnati Ave. In 0.4 mile turn left onto S. Miami Ave., and turn left again into the parking lot at Xenia Station (150 Miami Ave.) in 0.4 mile.

To reach the northernmost parking area in Springfield: From I-70, take Exit 54 and turn right onto OH 72/S. Limestone St. Travel 1.9 miles north (note that, to stay on Limestone, you need to bear left at the intersection with Selma Road), and turn left onto E. Pleasant St. Take the first right onto S. Fountain Ave. In 0.2 mile, turn left at W. Jefferson St., where you will find parking. The trail begins near the opposite (west) end of the parking lot at the intersection of Jefferson and Center Sts.

The Midtown Greenway is a relatively short, but vital, 5.5-mile link that provides a direct crosstown route for recreation and bike commuting in south Minneapolis. Most of the trail is below grade, a result of the former railroad being mandated to sink the tracks, which today offers a safe corridor separating trail users from busy streets. Combined with few road crossings, links to numerous other trails that travel throughout the city and suburbs, plowing service in the winter, and 24-7 well-lit access, the Greenway is just one example of why Minneapolis is consistently ranked one of the top bike cities in the United States.

The trail's smart design incorporates westbound and eastbound biking lanes, as well as a separate walking path.

View of the 12th Avenue bridge from the trail

County
Hennepin

Endpoints
W. River Pkwy. and
E. 27th St. to just north
of W. Lake St. (near
Chowen Ave. S), where
it connects to the Cedar
Lake LRT Regional Trail
(Minneapolis)

Mileage
5.5

Roughness Index
1

Surface
Asphalt

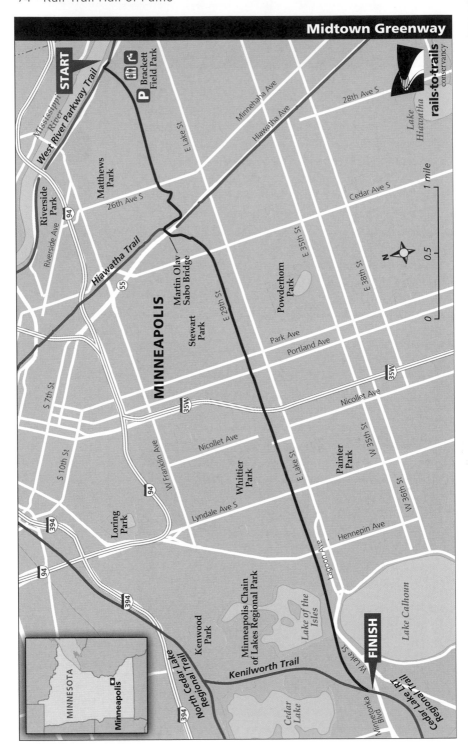

The Midtown Greenway traverses a lush, tree-lined corridor, as shown in this view from the 13th Avenue bridge.

Although this "bike freeway" is undeniably urban, it is also lush and green. The walls to either side of the trail are sloped and filled with trees, bushes, and organic vegetation built up over a century. Annual Arbor Day celebrations have also added thousands more trees.

At its eastern end, the trail begins near the Mississippi River, which also provides a connection to the West River Parkway Trail. Considered a rail-with-trail, this first section of the Greenway follows an active rail line, with a fence separating the two corridors. Farther along, find one of the unique features of the Greenway, the Martin Olav Sabo Bridge. Available only to trail users, this cable-stayed suspension bridge rises majestically 220 feet over Hiawatha Avenue, with the cable-stay tower cutting a dramatic figure 100 feet above the bridge-level deck.

The Greenway runs one block north and parallel to Lake Street, an area with many shops, restaurants, and other amenities, and passes through several different neighborhoods. Along the way, find a trailside bike shop and community gardens, and pass under a series of bridges carrying street traffic. The route continues westward to its end in the Chain of Lakes, a district formed as a series of parks surrounding some of the city's most beautiful lakes. The path passes between Lake of the Isles and Lake Calhoun before reaching an intersection with the Cedar Lake LRT Regional Trail and the Kenilworth Trail (access is 0.25 mile east of Chowen Avenue).

RAIL-TRAIL HALL OF FAME SELECTION

Joining the Hall of Fame in 2015, the Midtown Greenway is a well-loved and well-used urban trail that provides a safe and efficient means of traversing Minneapolis, as well as connecting diverse neighborhoods and linking to other routes in the city's excellent multiuse trail network.

RAILROAD HISTORY

In 1882 the Greenway's corridor was constructed as part of the Milwaukee Railroad's main line to the west coast. At the time, this area was on the outskirts of the city, but, as Minneapolis grew, it was mandated that a trench be built to provide a grade separation between the rail line and streets to avoid conflicts at the many street crossings. By the early 1990s rail traffic had greatly diminished, leading to the eventual removal of tracks along a large section of the route.

CONTACT: midtowngreenway.org

DIRECTIONS

Much of the Midtown Greenway lies in a railroad trench below street level; access ramps are available at several points along the north side of the trail. You won't find dedicated trail parking, but street parking is readily available near the trail's access points.

To access parking at Brackett Field Park, take I-94 E to Exit 235A toward Riverside Ave./25th Ave. Merge onto S. Ninth St. and then immediately turn right onto 26th Ave. S. In 0.5 mile turn left onto E. 25th St., and in 0.7 mile turn right onto 36th Ave. S. Go 0.4 mile to E. 28th St., and in 0.2 mile turn left onto S. 39th Ave. to reach Brackett Field Park.

The Greenway can be accessed from the following locations: Calhoun Village Shopping Area, Dean Pkwy., Lake of the Isles Pkwy., James Ave. S, Irving Ave. S, Humboldt Ave. S, Bryant Ave. S, Nicollet Ave., Fifth Ave. S, Park Ave. S, 10th Ave. S, 11th Ave. S (the only wheelchair-accessible ramp along the route), 13th Ave. S, 18th Ave. S, E. 28th St., Hiawatha Ave., Minnehaha Ave., 26th Ave. S, 27th Ave. S, 29th Ave. S, 30th Ave. S, and W. River Pkwy.

Since 1999, when the first few miles of the Monon Trail were completed in Indianapolis, the route has been wildly successful—so much so that residents in Carmel, north of the trail's then-endpoint, demanded that they too should have the benefits of this incredible resource. Trail advocates organized, elected a pro-trail candidate on the city council, and built the extension (this section is locally known as the Monon Greenway). Today, the 27.1-mile route sees an incredible 1.4 million users a year, and the Monon now extends farther north to Sheridan.

The impressive Monon Trail begins in a rather unimpressive way near a snarl of interstate ramps just north of downtown Indianapolis. While this may not be the most picturesque start, it is a reminder that this is at its core an urban trail connecting the city with northern suburbs. The

The rail-trail features a few unique red bridges.

Counties
Hamilton, Marion

Endpoints
E. 10th St. at Lewis St. (Indianapolis) to Opel St. and E. 236th St. (Sheridan)

Mileage
27.1

Roughness Index
1

Surface
Asphalt

Monon Trail

SHERIDAN
W 236th St
FINISH P Legion Park
38
W 216th St
W 216th St
Mule Barn Rd
Six Points Rd
N Michigan Rd
31
HORTONVILLE
Horton Rd
421
Grand Park
38
BOONE COUNTY
HAMILTON COUNTY
Midland Trace Trail
W 176th St
WESTFIELD
NOBLESVILLE
32
32
Oak Ridge Rd
E 161st St
Cool Creek Park
Gray Rd
Hazel Dell Rd
31
E 146th St
P 🚻 ♿
Meadowlark Park
Hagan-Burke Trail
CARMEL
Towne Rd
31
ZIONSVILLE
Spring Mill Rd
The Monon Community Center
FISHERS
421
P 🚻 ♿
HAMILTON COUNTY
69
465
MARION COUNTY
P
CASTLETON
465
465
WILLIAMS CREEK
MERIDIAN HILLS
Marott Park
P
NORTH CROWS NEST
Opti Park
Broad Ripple Park
Fort Harrison State Park
Eagle Creek Reservoir
W 56th St
Central Canal Towpath
CROWS NEST
P 🚻
LAWRENCE
65
SPRING HILLS
WYNNEDALE
White River
N College Ave
Fall Creek Trail
36
465
465
38th St
74
North Park
E 30th St
70
SPEEDWAY
70
70
White River Wapahani Trail
65
P Hill Park
N
START
0 1 2 3 miles
INDIANAPOLIS
70
Indianapolis Cultural Trail
rails·to·trails
conservancy

Indianapolis
INDIANA

A bright-red bridge welcomes trail users to the village of Broad Ripple.

location also serves as a convenient link to another Indy trail success story, the Indianapolis Cultural Trail, which begins directly across 10th Street and travels through five cultural districts within the city.

Heading north on the Monon, pass through residential and industrial neighborhoods before reaching the Indiana State Fairgrounds. Enjoy a greener landscape as the trail travels through a section lined with trees and artwork from the local community. At mile marker 11, reach Broad Ripple Avenue. Stop to explore the many galleries, shops, and restaurants in this vibrant artistic village, and visit the Indianapolis Art Center, just a block off the trail on 67th Street.

Just beyond Broad Ripple is the 102-acre Marott Park, which includes a nature preserve with walking trails, and the White River, an ideal spot to cool your toes on a hot day. In Carmel, find the Monon Community Center, which features a skate park and a water park, complete with a lazy river, a variety of slides, and concessions. Spend time exploring the charming shops and restaurants along Main Street in Carmel before heading north to Westfield.

A pedestrian bridge over 146th Street marks your entrance to the city. Here you'll find a junction with another rail-trail, the Midland Trace Trail. Though you're still not out of the Indianapolis metro area, the Monon passes woodlots and farms on the north side of town on its way to Sheridan. The trail ends near the intersection of Opel and 236th Streets; a small parking lot marks the spot.

RAIL-TRAIL HALL OF FAME SELECTION

Inducted into the Hall of Fame in 2009, the Monon Trail set the bar for what an urban rail-trail should be. This busy nonmotorized route allows for a safe car-free link to downtown Indianapolis attractions, suburban neighborhoods, parks, and other sites, and it is a valuable resource for the communities it passes through.

RAILROAD HISTORY

Originally built as a rail corridor in the mid-1800s by the Chicago, Indianapolis, & Louisville Railroad, and known as the Monon, this north–south route was an important supply line for Union troops during the Civil War. Later, the railroad transported coal and freight before offering passenger service twice a day between Indianapolis and Chicago. Often called the Hoosier Line, and featuring cars bearing Indiana University colors and freight engines bearing Purdue University colors, the route, then owned by CSX Transportation, eventually fell into disuse.

CONTACT: bikethemonon.com

DIRECTIONS

Trailhead access is available in downtown Indianapolis and Carmel, as well as additional areas along the route.

On the southern end of the trail in Indianapolis, parking is available in Frank and Judy O'Bannon Old Northside Soccer Park (950 E. 16th St.). To reach the park: From I-70 E, take Exit 111 for Washington St.; turn left onto Washington. In 0.2 mile, turn right onto College Ave.; travel north 1.5 miles, then turn right onto E. 16th St. In 0.2 mile, you'll see the park entrance and parking on your right at the Bundy Pl. intersection; the Monon Trail parallels the east side of the park.

To reach the Westfield trailhead at the northern end of the trail: From I-465, take Exit 31 to US 31. Follow US 31 N for 7.7 miles, and take the exit for IN 32 W/Main St. Keep left to get on IN 32 W, and continue on the highway 0.9 mile. Turn left onto Dartown Road and drive 0.1 mile until the short road ends at Quaker Park (17501 Dartown Road), which will be on your left. Another trail, the Midland Trace, begins at the parking lot; take that 0.5 mile to the Monon Trail.

On the northern end of the trail in Sheridan, parking is available along Biddle Memorial Park (610 E. 10th St.). To reach the park: From I-465, take Exit 31 to US 31. Follow US 31 N for 11.4 miles, and take Exit 136, following signs for Sheridan. Turn left onto IN 38 W. Go 5.2 miles to IN 47 (E. 10th St.) and turn left. Continue on IN 47 for 0.3 mile to Opel St., and turn left into the parking area.

Nestled among aspens, maples, and oaks, and featuring stunning views of several of Minnesota's many lakes, is the 119-mile Paul Bunyan State Trail (PBST). This paved route immerses you in the quiet beauty of the north-central woodland region of the state while passing through welcoming small towns that cater to trail users by offering numerous amenities, including shuttle services. For those looking for a multiday adventure, the PBST connects to several other trails that travel for miles throughout the region, including up to the Canadian border.

Begin at the southern end of the PBST in Crow Wing State Park in Brainerd. Heading north, catch glimpses of the Mississippi River and pass through several towns as you wind through the scenic Brainerd Lakes Area, a popular recreational and resort destination. Throughout the

Enjoy the peace and quiet as you ride through this woodland beauty.

Counties
Beltrami, Cass, Crow Wing, Hubbard

Endpoints
Crow Wing State Park near N. Koering Road and MN 371 (Brainerd) to County Road 20 at Lake Bemidji State Park (Bemidji)

Mileage
119.3

Roughness Index
1

Surface
Asphalt

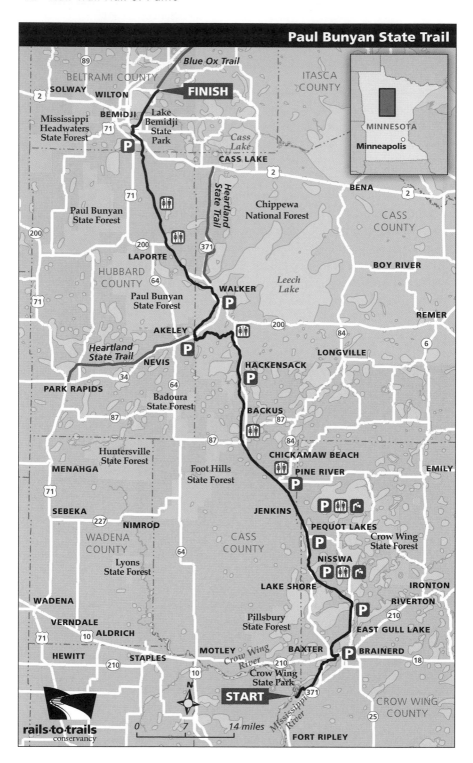

Paul Bunyan State Trail

Blue Ox Trail

FINISH

BELTRAMI COUNTY

ITASCA COUNTY

SOLWAY   2

WILTON

BEMIDJI

Lake Bemidji State Park

Cass Lake

MINNESOTA

Minneapolis

Mississippi Headwaters State Forest   71   P

CASS LAKE

2

BENA   2

71

Paul Bunyan State Forest

Heartland State Trail

Chippewa National Forest

CASS COUNTY

200

200

LAPORTE

371

BOY RIVER

HUBBARD COUNTY   64

Leech Lake

REMER   6

71

Paul Bunyan State Forest

WALKER   P

LONGVILLE

84

AKELEY   P

200

Heartland State Trail

NEVIS

34   64

HACKENSACK   P

PARK RAPIDS

Badoura State Forest

BACKUS

87

87

84

87

Huntersville State Forest

Foot Hills State Forest

CHICKAMAW BEACH

PINE RIVER   P

EMILY

MENAHGA

71

JENKINS

P

SEBEKA

227

NIMROD

PEQUOT LAKES   P

Crow Wing State Forest

WADENA COUNTY

CASS COUNTY

64

Lyons State Forest

NISSWA   P

IRONTON

LAKE SHORE

RIVERTON

WADENA

P

210

VERNDALE

10   ALDRICH

71

Pillsbury State Forest

EAST GULL LAKE

HEWITT

210

MOTLEY

STAPLES

Crow Wing River

BAXTER   210

P   BRAINERD   18

10

N

START

Crow Wing State Park

371

CROW WING COUNTY

25

Mississippi River

FORT RIPLEY

rails·to·trails
conservancy

0   7   14 miles

Along the journey, you will find towns situated every 8–10 miles.

route, see various sites that pay homage to Paul Bunyan and Babe the Blue Ox. In Pequot Lakes you can relax in Paul's chair at Bobber Park; in Pine River you can stand in his wooden baby shoes; and in Hackensack you can see a 17-foot-high fiberglass statue of his girlfriend, Lucette (this is also the site of a popular annual chainsaw carving festival).

Farther north, you'll come to a Y in the trail. Head left toward Chippewa National Forest. This slightly hilly route provides a stunning backdrop of old-growth forest with trees that are more than 350 years old and are home to bald eagles, several species of hawks, woodpeckers, and many other animals. Here you will also find an intersection with the 49-mile Heartland State Trail, which shares a corridor with the PBST through the town of Walker. With numerous services and amenities, including more than 21 campgrounds in Chippewa National Forest (as well as 1,300 lakes and streams), the area offers an ideal base for exploration of the PBST. Turn right at the Y to connect to the 6.8-mile Shingobee Connection Trail that travels to Walker, reconnecting with the PBST but bypassing the hilly section through Chippewa. North of town, the Heartland State Trail splits off and the PBST heads northwest.

Cross the Kabekona River and continue on toward the trail's end in Bemidji, about 37 miles away. With the headwaters of the Mississippi River nearby, this is the first city along the river and home to Lake Bemidji State Park, where ambitious riders can continue on a 17-mile loop around the lake or connect to the nearly 100-mile-long Blue Ox Trail, which continues north to the Canadian border.

RAIL-TRAIL HALL OF FAME SELECTION

Inducted into the Hall of Fame in 2011, the Paul Bunyan State Trail is one of the longest rail-trails in the country. It offers a spectacular journey on a well-maintained route that showcases the beauty and quiet majesty of Minnesota. With classic lake vistas and dense forests home to a wide array of wildlife, the trail provides an ideal family-friendly adventure.

RAILROAD HISTORY

In the late 1800s a 12-mile section of the corridor that the PBST now follows began as a logging railroad built by the Gull River Lumber Company. By 1896 the route had been taken over by the Brainerd & Northern Minnesota Railway, and the line from Brainerd to Bemidji was established. The railway was very successful, mainly transporting timber but also passengers who came to the many lake resorts in the region. By the 1980s, however, business had declined, and Burlington Northern Railway stopped operations.

CONTACT: dnr.state.mn.us/state_trails/paul_bunyan

DIRECTIONS

Parking and access for the Paul Bunyan State Trail is available in every town along the way.

To reach the southern trailhead at Crow Wing State Park, from the intersection of MN 210 and MN 371 in Baxter, take MN 371 S for 7.5 miles to 60th Ave. SW/N. Koering Road. Follow it northwest 1.3 miles through Crow Wing State Park to the parking lot, which will be on your right.

To reach the parking lot in Baxter, from the intersection of MN 210 and MN 371 in Baxter, go north one block on MN 371 to Excelsior Road. Turn right onto Excelsior and go 0.75 mile to Conservation Dr.; the parking lot is on the left.

The northern trailhead is located in Lake Bemidji State Park. From the intersection of US 71 and US 2/MN 197/Paul Bunyan Dr. in Bemidji, head east on Paul Bunyan Dr. for 1.6 miles. Turn left onto Bemidji Ave. N, and go 3.9 miles. Turn right onto Birchmont Beach Road/County Road 20, and go 1.5 miles to the park's entrance. Follow State Park Road 1 mile to the trailhead.

Located in central Michigan, the 30-mile paved Pere Marquette Rail-Trail (PMRT) offers a family-friendly recreational corridor through pastoral countryside and charming small towns. An extremely well-maintained route with a dedicated group of volunteers, the rail-trail is a popular destination for locals and visitors alike.

Begin at the Tridge. This unique three-way wooden bridge features one pillar and three spokes that span the confluence of the Chippewa and Tittabawassee Rivers in downtown Midland. From the bridge, access the 4-mile Chippewa Trail, which heads to the Chippewa Nature Center; explore the downtown; or visit two surrounding parks. Head north to follow the PMRT.

As you leave Midland behind, come upon the Alden B. Dow Home & Studio. This remarkable mid-century

The rail-trail offers a serene experience through nature, with small towns within easy reach.

Counties
Clare, Isabella, Midland

Endpoints
Chippewa Trail at the Tridge near Crissey and Towsley Sts. (Midland) to Pine and E. Fourth Sts. (Clare)

Mileage
30.0

Roughness Index
1

Surface
Asphalt

Pere Marquette Rail-Trail

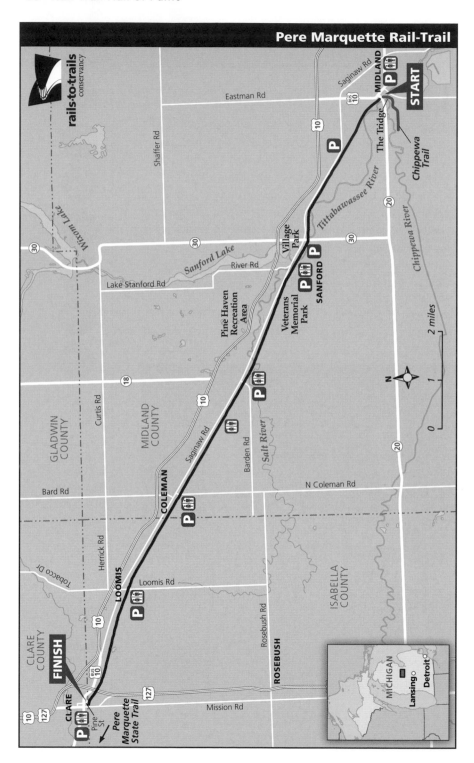

Travelers will experience rural central Michigan along this route.

home, set among stunning grounds just off the trail, is considered one of the top historical homes in the country. Also nearby, visit the 110-acre Dow Gardens; the Dow Historical Museum, which includes information about the history of chemical experiments by Herbert H. Dow; and the restored 1874 Bradley House, which gives a glimpse into the life of a family during that period in time. (Note that some sites require reservations.) Farther along at the 8.5-mile marker, reach the town of Sanford. Stop to explore Village Park, located on Sanford Lake; visit the Sanford Centennial Museum, which includes several historical buildings with memorabilia and artifacts that chronicle local history; or grab a bite at one of several restaurants in town.

Northwest of Sanford, pass by Veterans Memorial Park and Pine Haven Recreation Area. Depending on the time of year, this beautiful rolling country-side may be full of colorful wildflowers. In Coleman, find several restaurants as well as a bike shop. (An adjacent equestrian path also runs about 5 miles between Coleman and MI 18/North Castor Road.)

There are numerous access points along the trail, as well as benches for trail users to rest and take in the beautiful scenery of maple and pine trees. The path continues approximately another 10 miles before ending in Clare.

In Clare, connect to the 57-mile Pere Marquette State Trail, located 1.5 miles away. To reach it, head north on Pine Street and take a left onto East Fourth Street. Take a right onto Maple Street and a left onto Main Street. Follow Main west out of town until you see the trailhead and parking lot on the left side of the road (note that Main Street is a busy road). This route passes through spectacular countryside of woodlands and wetlands along a crushed limestone trail. At the trail's end in Reed City, connect to the 92-mile Fred Meijer White Pine Trail State Park.

RAIL-TRAIL HALL OF FAME SELECTION

The Pere Marquette Rail-Trail, added to the Rail-Trail Hall of Fame in 2009, is a well-loved route that attracts visitors from far and wide. Packed with interesting natural and historical sites, and offering the opportunity to connect to additional trails, this flat and easy route truly offers something for everyone.

RAILROAD HISTORY

The corridor of the PMRT was established over the course of several years in the mid- to late 1800s by the Flint & Pere Marquette Railway (it later merged with two separate railroads to become the Pere Marquette Railroad). The PMRT route operated under the Ludington Division and ran from Saginaw across the state to Ludington on Lake Michigan, hauling timber and other products, as well as connecting to the lucrative car ferries that traveled across the lake to Wisconsin. Eventually, the Pere Marquette was acquired by the Chesapeake & Ohio Railroad and became inactive in the 1980s.

CONTACT: peremarquetterailtrail.org

DIRECTIONS

Trailheads are available at towns along the route.

To reach the southern trailhead in Midland: From I-75, take Exit 162B (US 10), and follow US 10 W for 11.2 miles. Take Exit 128 for US 10 Bus. to downtown Midland. Continue on US 10 Bus. for 3.8 miles (it will become Patrick St. and then Indian St.), and turn left onto Ashman St. After 0.4 mile, Ashman will dead-end in a roundabout with the Midland Farmers Market pavilion in the center; here you'll find parking, restrooms, and the trailhead.

To reach the northern trailhead in Clare: From Lansing, take US 127 N for 81.1 miles, and take Exit 156 (US 127 Bus.). Follow US 127 Bus. for 1.2 miles, and turn right onto E. Fourth St. The trail begins in one block at the corner of Fourth and Pine Sts. Street parking is available along both Fourth and Pine Sts.

19 Prairie Spirit Trail State Park

Traversing a variety of landscapes—including tallgrass prairie, riparian zones, and farmland—and passing through 10 small towns, the Prairie Spirit Trail State Park (PST) offers a glimpse into the spirit of Kansas. The route, stretching just more than 51 miles, heads south from Ottawa to Iola, with connections to other trails that travel for miles throughout the state.

Begin your journey in Ottawa at the Old Depot Museum. Located at the trailhead, the museum was a gift of the Atchison, Topeka & Santa Fe Railway in 1962, and, in addition to being an interesting structure, it chronicles the history of this former railroad town.

As you head south, the trail becomes crushed stone (it is paved in small sections in Ottawa, Garnett, and Iola)

The trail immerses travelers in the bucolic scenery of rural eastern Kansas.

Counties
Allen, Anderson, Franklin

Endpoints
Tecumseh St. west of
N. Main St. (Ottawa) to
Southwind Rail Trail at
W. Bruner St. west of
S. State St. (Iola)

Mileage
51.3

Roughness Index
1

Surface
Asphalt, Crushed Stone

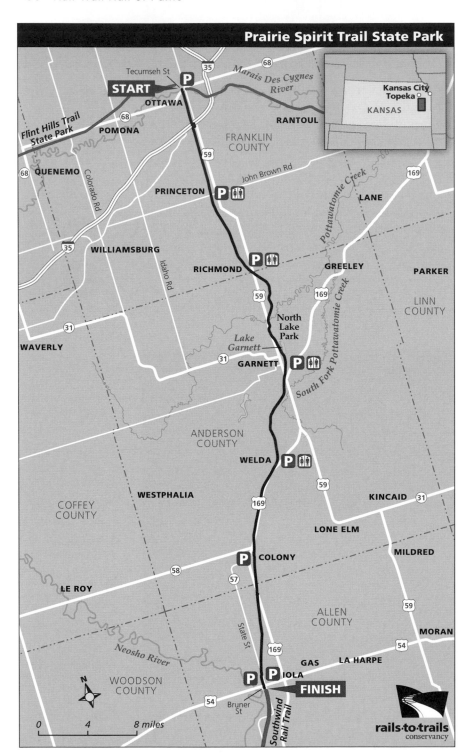

Prairie Spirit Trail State Park

The path connects 10 charming small towns

and intersects with the 117-mile Flint Hills Trail State Park. At the midpoint in Garnett, enjoy another railroad relic at the restored 1932 Santa Fe Depot, which provides a welcoming rest stop with amenities and displays of various pieces of railroad memorabilia.

The PST immerses trail users in the bucolic scenery of rural eastern Kansas and features an abundance of prairie landscapes and, depending on the season, meadows of wildflowers and bushes full of blackberries, wild strawberries, and Chickasaw plums, which attract a wide variety of bird species. The area south of Garnett is home to a native prairie reserve that protects the rare Mead's milkweed and other endangered species of the tallgrass prairie. Also find welcome shade in stands of such hardwoods as hickory and oak, pass over several bridges, and stop to dip your toes in the Marais Des Cygnes River and Pottawatomie Creek.

At the PST's endpoint in the small town of Iola, enjoy amenities and restaurants, as well as the Allen County Historical Society Museum (20 S. Washington St.). This small museum has a variety of exhibits, images, and artifacts that tell the history of this town; it's worth a short visit.

Here you can also make a seamless transition to the 6.5-mile Southwind Rail Trail.

RAIL-TRAIL HALL OF FAME SELECTION

Inducted into the Hall of Fame in 2011, the Prairie Spirit Trail State Park highlights the natural beauty of eastern Kansas and showcases the region's rich history along a well-maintained corridor. The rail-trail is ideal for families or for adventurers looking for a multiday exploration via connections with other trails.

RAILROAD HISTORY

The Leavenworth, Lawrence, & Fort Gibson Railroad operated a north-south rail line through Kansas that, by 1871, included the corridor that the PSRT now follows. By the end of the decade, the line was sold to the Atchison, Topeka & Santa Fe Railway. In addition to serving the agricultural industry, the *Tulsan,* a passenger train powered by streamlined diesels, provided service from 1939 and offered such luxuries as a diner car and a parlor-observation car. The *Tulsan* made its final run in 1971, while the rail line continued operations until 1990.

CONTACT: ksoutdoors.com/state-parks/locations/prairie-spirit-trail

DIRECTIONS

Trailheads are available at towns along the route.

To reach the northern trailhead in Ottawa: From I-35, take Exit 187 for KS 68. Travel 2 miles west on KS 68 to reach Ottawa (as you approach town, the highway becomes Logan St.), and take a left onto Main St. In 0.1 mile, take a right onto Tecumseh St. and look for the Old Depot Museum (135 W. Tecumseh St.) on your right. Park in the lot adjacent to the museum; the trail begins just across the street from the parking lot.

To reach the southern trailhead in Iola: From I-35, take Exit 155 (US 75), and follow US 75 S for 38.1 miles. Turn left onto US 54 E/W. Mary St., and go 18.7 miles. Turn right onto W. Davis St., and in 0.2 mile, turn left onto W. Bruner St. The parking lot will be on your left, and the trailhead is just west of the lot.

Nestled in the southwestern corner of Iowa, the nearly 63-mile Wabash Trace Nature Trail (WTNT) travels through a remarkable landscape that is home to a diverse array of flora, including some plant species that are found nowhere else in the state. From the Missouri border north to Council Bluffs, Iowa, the trail offers sweeping views through scenic countryside with a shaded tree canopy for part of the route.

Before setting out on the WTNT, trail users should visit **wabashtrace.org** to check conditions (sections can get washed out after heavy storms) and to ensure that no events are taking place at the time of a planned visit. The WTNT hosts the Wabash Trace Nature Trail Marathon, as well as a 10-mile Thursday night Taco Ride, the longest-running weekly bike ride in the country. Also note that

A former railroad bridge is just one of many highlights of the nearly 63-mile trail.

Counties
Fremont, Mills, Page, Pottawattamie

Endpoints
Iowa–Missouri state line near N. Railroad St. and E. Main St. (Blanchard) to Iowa West Foundation Trailhead Park at E. South Omaha Bridge Road near Harry Langdon Blvd. (Council Bluffs)

Mileage
62.6

Roughness Index
2

Surface
Asphalt, Concrete, Crushed Stone

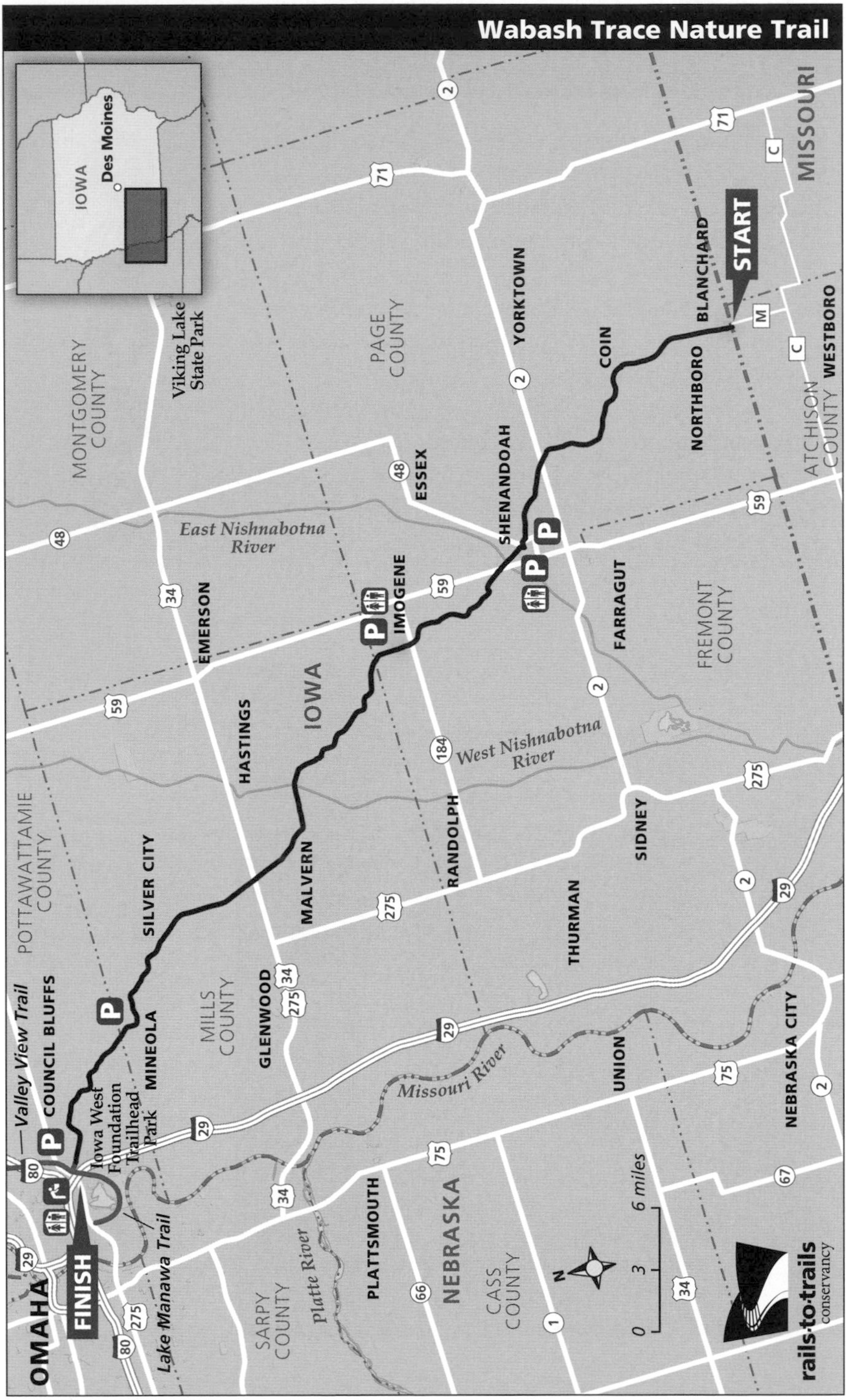

Wabash Trace Nature Trail

IOWA
Des Moines
MISSOURI

71
c
MISSOURI
2
BLANCHARD
START
M
71
YORKTOWN
NORTHBORO
WESTBORO
2
COIN
c
PAGE COUNTY
ATCHISON COUNTY
59
ESSEX
48
SHENANDOAH
East Nishnabotna River
P P
FARRAGUT
MONTGOMERY COUNTY
Viking Lake State Park
34
EMERSON
59
IMOGENE
P
FREMONT COUNTY
48
HASTINGS
IOWA
West Nishnabotna River
184
275
59
RANDOLPH
SIDNEY
POTTAWATTAMIE COUNTY
SILVER CITY
MALVERN
275
THURMAN
2
29
Valley View Trail
COUNCIL BLUFFS
MINEOLA
GLENWOOD
34
275
UNION
NEBRASKA CITY
75
2
P
Iowa West Foundation Trailhead Park
MILLS COUNTY
Missouri River
29
80
P
29
75
67
FINISH
Lake Manawa Trail
34
PLATTSMOUTH
NEBRASKA
CASS COUNTY
OMAHA
29
SARPY COUNTY
Platte River
66
1
80
275
N
0   3   6 miles
34

rails-to-trails
conservancy

The trail passes through several small towns, which offer trailheads and amenities.

the trail is largely maintained by volunteers, and a $2 daily trail pass is highly encouraged and easily purchased at drop boxes located at trailheads.

Take advantage of a slight downhill grade by beginning at the southern trailhead in Blanchard. As you bike along this rural trail, pass through a wide-open prairie landscape and enjoy a seemingly endless vista unencumbered by any major development. The WTNT passes through several small towns, all of which have trailheads and offer a variety of amenities for trail users (short sections in towns have an asphalt or concrete surface; otherwise, the route is crushed stone).

As you reach the northern section of the WTNT, enter the Loess Hills. Formed by deposits of fine windblown soil, spanning 15 miles and nearly 200 miles long, this distinctive geological feature is one of the highest hills made of loess in the world (the highest is in China). The hills were formed at the end of the last glacial period, and, from the rich topsoil that evolved, an ecosystem developed that was accommodating to ice age animals, such as woolly mammoths, giant sloths, and camels, as well as to early humans. Today, this environment is home to unique plant life, including the skeleton plant and prairie moonwort, and is an important habitat for prairie wildlife, including red-tailed hawks. Pass through this unusual landscape as you head toward the trail's end in Council Bluffs (the last 4 miles also feature an adjacent equestrian path). From here, the WTNT links to the 7-mile Valley View Trail and the 7.5-mile Lake Manawa Trail.

Nearly the entire route offers a pleasant, shaded tree canopy.

RAIL-TRAIL HALL OF FAME SELECTION

The Wabash Trace Nature Trail is one of Iowa's premier rail-trails. The route offers a scenic ride through the quiet rural countryside and also traverses the dramatic and unusual Loess Hills, a destination in and of itself. The rail-trail was inducted into the Hall of Fame in 2011.

RAILROAD HISTORY

The Wabash Trace corridor was established by the Wabash Railroad during the 1870s and was an important connection between Midwestern farmlands, factories, and small towns. At its peak, the railroad had a network covering more than 2,000 miles and became well known due to the popular 1900s folk song "The Wabash Cannonball." In later years, a passenger train by this name was established that connected St. Louis to Detroit. In the 1960s, the railroad was folded into the Norfolk and Western Railway. In the 1980s, as business declined, the Council Bluffs route became inactive.

CONTACT: **wabashtrace.org**

DIRECTIONS

Trailheads can be found at several of the towns along the route.

To reach the southern trailhead: From I-29, take Exit 2 (IA 2). Head east 7.2 miles on IA 2, and continue straight 13.4 miles on County Road J46/250th St. Turn right onto US 59 S, and go 2 miles. Turn left onto 270th St., and go 8.5 miles. Turn right onto Hackberry Ave., and go 5.2 miles to Blanchard. Continue straight on Second St. for 0.2 mile, and turn right onto Main St. The street dead-ends at the trail in 0.2 mile. There is no trailhead parking, so park along Main St.

In Council Bluffs, there is abundant parking at the trailhead. From I-29 S, take Exit 47 for IA 92 E. Follow IA 92 E for 0.7 mile, and turn right onto Harry Langdon Blvd. In another 0.7 mile, turn right onto E. South Omaha Bridge Road, which will take you into Iowa West Foundation Trailhead Park. The trail begins in the park.

Enjoy views of prairie landscapes and rural farmland along the path.

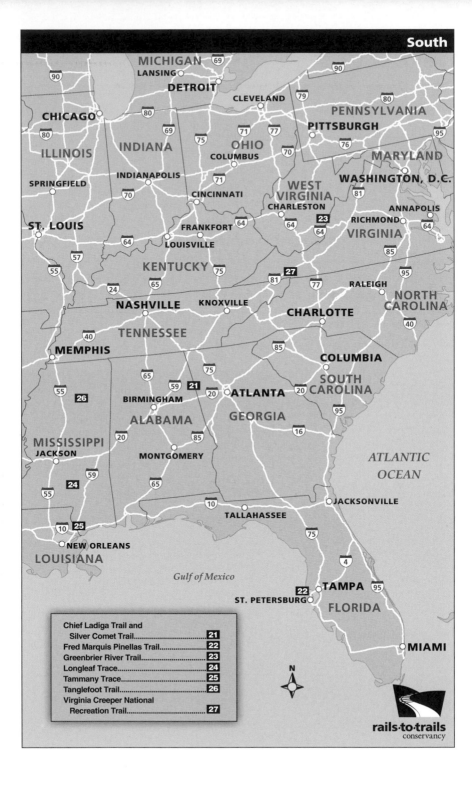

South

MICHIGAN 69
LANSING
DETROIT
CLEVELAND 79
80
PENNSYLVANIA
CHICAGO 80
PITTSBURGH
95
69 75 71 77 76
ILLINOIS INDIANA OHIO MARYLAND
80 COLUMBUS 70

SPRINGFIELD INDIANAPOLIS 71 WASHINGTON, D.C.
70 CINCINNATI WEST 81
VIRGINIA
CHARLESTON ANNAPOLIS
ST. LOUIS FRANKFORT 64 64 23 RICHMOND
64 64 VIRGINIA 64
LOUISVILLE
57 85
55 KENTUCKY 75 27 95
24 65 81 77 RALEIGH NORTH
CAROLINA
NASHVILLE KNOXVILLE CHARLOTTE 40
40 TENNESSEE
MEMPHIS 85 COLUMBIA

65 75 SOUTH
55 26 59 21 20 CAROLINA
BIRMINGHAM 20 ATLANTA 20
ALABAMA GEORGIA 95
MISSISSIPPI 20 85 16
JACKSON ATLANTIC
MONTGOMERY OCEAN
59
55 24 65
10 JACKSONVILLE
TALLAHASSEE
10 25 75
NEW ORLEANS
LOUISIANA Gulf of Mexico 4

TAMPA 95
22
ST. PETERSBURG FLORIDA

Chief Ladiga Trail and
Silver Comet Trail........................... 21
Fred Marquis Pinellas Trail.............. 22
Greenbrier River Trail...................... 23
Longleaf Trace................................ 24
Tammany Trace............................... 25
Tanglefoot Trail.............................. 26
Virginia Creeper National
Recreation Trail............................ 27

MIAMI

N

rails·to·trails
conservancy

Much of the Virginia Creeper National Recreation Trail parallels Whitetop Laurel Creek (see page 126).

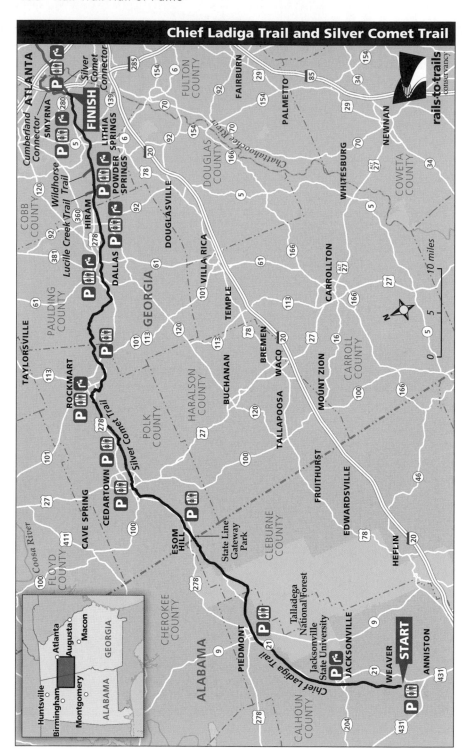

For recreational biking enthusiasts, the Chief Ladiga and Silver Comet Trails are about as close to perfection as you can get in an off-road route. With a combined 94 miles, this is one of the longest paved rail-trails in the country, passing through two states and numerous small towns. The trails provide a tranquil, stress-free environment, with beautiful natural surroundings and few road crossings within easy reach of downtown Atlanta, situated about 15 miles from the Silver Comet's eastern endpoint. Along the way, there are several trail-adjacent diversions, including a popular lake for a quick and refreshing swim, walking paths, and historical railroad sites.

Begin in Anniston, Alabama, on the Chief Ladiga Trail, named for a Muscogee tribe leader. Pass through such towns as Weaver and Jacksonville, where the route goes through the heart of Jacksonville State University and the quaint town of Piedmont. Cross several bridges and restored railroad trestles, and keep your eyes open for wildlife, such as deer, fox, and many bird species, as you skirt the Terrapin Creek and ride into the Talladega

The Chief Ladiga Trail travels along and over Terrapin Creek.

Counties
AL: Calhoun, Cleburne;
GA: Cobb, Paulding, Polk

Endpoints
Holley Farm and Weaver Roads (Anniston, AL) to Mavell Road near Creekside Pl. SE (Smyrna, GA); the two trails meet at State Line Gateway Park on the Alabama–Georgia state line (near County Roads 49 and 239 in Piedmont, AL, and near Shiloh and Hardin Roads in Esom Hill, GA)

Mileage
94.5 combined
(Chief Ladiga: 33.0;
Silver Comet: 61.5)

Roughness Index
1

Surface
Asphalt, Concrete

The Silver Comet Trail winds through Heritage Park in Smyrna.

National Forest. Shortly afterward, enter State Line Gateway Park to make the seamless transition to Georgia's Silver Comet Trail.

In Cedartown, about 10 miles east of the Alabama–Georgia border, find trailside amenities as well as the Cedartown Depot, which now houses a small exhibit on the route's railroad history. Afterward, prepare for some hills, as this section has several inclines on your way to Rockmart, which offers several restaurants where you can rest. Just outside of town, find Coot's Lake, a popular local swimming spot and the perfect place to relax and cool down for a bit. This stretch also contains one of the more dramatic points on the route, the Pumpkinvine Trestle. Built in 1901, this bridge is more than 750 feet long and rises 126 feet over Pumpkinvine Creek.

At mile marker 8.6 (Carter Road), take a slight detour to bike 1.5 miles (3 miles round-trip) on the Wildhorse Trail. This paved spur that starts at the trailhead and runs along Wildhorse and Noses Creek has an observation tower that looks out over wetlands. Try to spot woodpeckers and thrashers, and observe bat and owl boxes hanging on some of the tall trees. Also keep your eyes open for Georgia's largest known red maple. Back on the trail, head toward the end of the route, just a short distance farther along in Smyrna.

Exciting plans are afoot to connect the eastern end of the Silver Comet Trail in Smyrna to downtown Atlanta via the Silver Comet Connector. This burgeoning pathway will also cross another important and developing rail-trail, the Atlanta Beltline, which will one day encircle the city. The connector trail is anticipated to be completed by 2022 or 2023. Another trail linkage emanating from the same starting point is already open; the Cumberland Connector begins at the eastern trailhead of the Silver Comet Trail and heads northeast, providing access to neighborhood amenities like Oakdale Park and Cumberland Mall.

RAIL-TRAIL HALL OF FAME SELECTION

In 1988, with assistance from Rails-to-Trails Conservancy, the 61.5-mile Silver Comet Trail began to take shape in Georgia—representing one of the first formal rail-trail development efforts in the South. The trail helped inspire many southern rail-trail efforts to come. In 2008 the Silver Comet was connected to the 33-mile Chief Ladiga Trail in Alabama, creating one of the longest rail-trails in the country. The trails were welcomed together into the Hall of Fame in 2009.

RAILROAD HISTORY

The Silver Comet Trail and Chief Ladiga Trail follow the route of the luxury passenger train *Silver Comet,* which was run by Seaboard Air Line and took passengers from New York City (via connections with other northern lines) to Birmingham, Alabama. The stainless steel streamliner train was a striking presence as it passed through this area 1947–1969, and it had such amenities as Pullman-service sleepers, lounges, and an observation coach. The rail corridor itself was in use long before the *Silver Comet,* dating from 1897, and was in continued operations until 1989, when the owners at the time, CSX Railroad, discontinued using the route.

CONTACT: silvercometga.com

DIRECTIONS

To reach the Anniston, Alabama, trailhead: From I-20, take Exit 185 and head north 6.6 miles through Anniston on AL 21/Quintard Ave. Bear right onto McClellan Blvd./AL 21 on the north side of town for 2 miles. Turn left onto Weaver Road; continue about a mile, and then turn left again onto Holley Farm Road to the well-marked Woodland Park trailhead.

To reach State Line Gateway Park: From I-20, take Exit 11 in Georgia. Follow US 27 N 20 miles. Turn left onto Youngs Farm Road, and in 1.4 miles turn left onto GA 100. In 1.1 miles bear right onto Lime Branch Road, which becomes Culp Lake Road in 1.7 miles. Continue 4.9 miles, and take a right onto Treat Mountain Road. In 0.3 mile turn left onto Shiloh Road. In 0.5 mile find the park at the Alabama–Georgia state line.

To reach the Smyrna, Georgia, trailhead: From I-285, take Exit 16 for Atlanta Road. Follow Atlanta Road northeast 0.4 mile, and turn left onto Cumberland Pkwy. SE. In 0.6 mile turn slightly right onto S. Cobb Dr. In 0.4 mile turn left onto Cooper Lake Road SE, and go 0.7 mile. Turn left onto Mavell Road, and go 0.3 mile to the trailhead parking.

Trailheads are also available in Weaver, Jacksonville, and Piedmont in Alabama and in Cedartown, Rockmart, and Dallas in Georgia, as well as at several other places along the route.

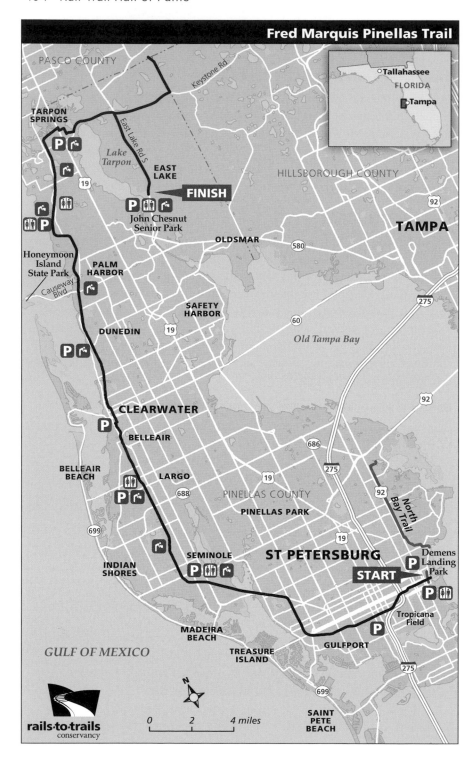

Fred Marquis Pinellas Trail

PASCO COUNTY

Keystone Rd

TARPON
SPRINGS

Lake
Tarpon

East Lake Rd S

19

EAST
LAKE

FINISH

John Chesnut
Senior Park

OLDSMAR

580

HILLSBOROUGH COUNTY

Honeymoon
Island
State Park

PALM
HARBOR

Causeway
Blvd

SAFETY
HARBOR

DUNEDIN

19

60

Old Tampa Bay

TAMPA

92

92

CLEARWATER

BELLEAIR

686

BELLEAIR
BEACH

LARGO

688

19

PINELLAS COUNTY

275

92

North Bay Trail

699

PINELLAS PARK

INDIAN
SHORES

SEMINOLE

ST PETERSBURG

19

Demens
Landing
Park

START

MADEIRA
BEACH

TREASURE
ISLAND

GULFPORT

Tropicana
Field

GULF OF MEXICO

275

N

699

SAINT
PETE
BEACH

rails·to·trails
conservancy

0   2   4 miles

FLORIDA

Tallahassee

Tampa

Stretching from St. Petersburg north past Tarpon Springs and inland to East Lake, the nearly 50-mile Fred Marquis Pinellas Trail (FMPT) is the ideal route to experience a slice of the Sunshine State. The trail passes through several small coastal towns, offers lovely Gulf Coast views, and allows easy access to scenic diversions.

Begin at the vibrant waterfront in St. Petersburg, just around the corner from some of the state's leading cultural institutions, including the Dali Museum and the Museum of Fine Arts. This area offers visitors a plethora of activities, shops, and restaurants, along with breathtaking harbor views. Unfortunately, as you begin heading north along the trail, you quickly experience some of the least picturesque portions of the route as it cuts through the urban heart of the city. Don't let this dissuade you, however, as you will soon leave the city behind.

Pass through Clearwater and Dunedin, both of which offer a variety of shops and restaurants. Just north of Dunedin, turn left onto Causeway Boulevard to take a

A pleasant trailside bench to take in the scenery

County
Pinellas

Endpoints
First Ave. S and Bayshore Dr. (St. Petersburg) to John Chesnut Sr. Park at East Lake Road S near Sandy Point Road (East Lake)

Mileage
49.8

Roughness Index
1

Surface
Asphalt

detour to Honeymoon Island State Park. Enjoy a scenic ride across the causeway, wander trails looking for osprey and other wildlife, visit the nature center, take a dip in the pristine gulf waters, and enjoy a bite at the beachside grill before heading back to the FMPT.

As you head north, the route is much more tranquil than the southern section, with fewer cross streets. In Tarpon Springs, experience a taste of old Florida in the quaint downtown, which is listed on the National Register of Historic Places. Slightly farther along, visit the famous Sponge Docks. The town has the highest percentage of Greek Americans in the country, many of whose ancestors came to the area for its sponge harvesting industry. To reach the docks, turn left onto Athens Street several blocks past the historic district and follow the road to the waterfront. Here you will find many shops selling sea sponges, as well as numerous Greek restaurants and bakeries, and you will have the opportunity to learn more about the sponge diving industry (which sadly was severely damaged in a 1947 red tide algae bloom).

From Tarpon Springs, the FMPT heads inland for 4.8 miles to East Lake Road South, where the trail splits. One branch turns south, paralleling East Lake Road South for 4.3 miles to John Chesnut Sr. Park, which has nature trails and a lookout tower with views over Lake Tarpon. The other forks east along Keystone Road, then turns north, ending at the Pasco County line.

Excitingly, the FMPT plays a role in two growing trail networks. One is the Pinellas County effort to create a 75-mile system of linked trails from Tarpon Springs to St. Petersburg called the Pinellas Trail Loop. The other is the Coast-to-Coast Connector Trail, a developing 250-mile route across Florida, stretching from the Gulf of Mexico in Pinellas County to the Atlantic Ocean on the eastern side of the state.

RAIL-TRAIL HALL OF FAME SELECTION

One of the first trails in the Hall of Fame, the Fred Marquis Pinellas Trail was inducted in 2007. The trail, which opened in 1996, connects some of the most highly urbanized areas of Pinellas County with parks, scenic coastal areas, and residential neighborhoods, making it an important facility for both transportation and health on Florida's west coast. It was first envisioned by a group dedicated to creating safer places for biking and walking in the area after a 17-year-old was killed while attempting to cross a causeway on his bike. The trail includes 10 overpasses and 3 underpasses constructed specifically to allow trail users to go above or beneath the route's busiest intersections.

RAILROAD HISTORY

The FMPT follows the rail corridor once traveled by the Seaboard Air Line and the Atlantic Coast Line. These lines contributed greatly to the economic development of the state, bringing vacationers south and minerals and produce north. This route, and all service to Florida, would be important to the railroad's success as well, since this previously untapped market proved incredibly profitable. Over time, however, other methods of transportation took over; after being acquired by CSX Transportation, this corridor eventually became inactive in 1984.

CONTACT: pinellascounty.org/trailgd

DIRECTIONS

To reach the southern trailhead at Demens Landing Park in St. Petersburg from I-275, take Exit 22 for I-175 E toward Tropicana Field. Continue on I-175 E 0.9 mile, and then merge onto Fifth Ave. S/Dali Blvd. In 0.3 mile turn left onto First St. SE and continue 0.3 mile. Turn right directly into the parking lot and trailhead.

To reach the trailhead at John Chesnut Sr. Park from St. Petersburg, take I-275 N to Exit 30 (FL 686 W/Roosevelt Blvd.), and follow signs for 118th Ave. N. Merge onto 118th Ave. N and go 0.8 mile to 49th St. N. Turn right. Continue on County Road 611/49th St. N nearly 13 miles, and turn left into John Chesnut Sr. Park just after the bridge over Brooker Creek. To reach the trailhead at John Chesnut Sr. Park from I-75, take Exit 275 to merge onto FL 56 W, and go 0.7 mile. Continue on FL 54 W 14 miles, and turn left onto Trinity Blvd. After 5.5 miles, turn left onto East Lake Road N, and continue 5.5 miles. Turn right into the park; the trailhead is immediately to your right. For parking, continue along the access road, and turn right. Look for the parking lot on your right.

Trailheads are also available in Clearwater, Dunedin, and Tarpon Springs, as well as at other points along the route.

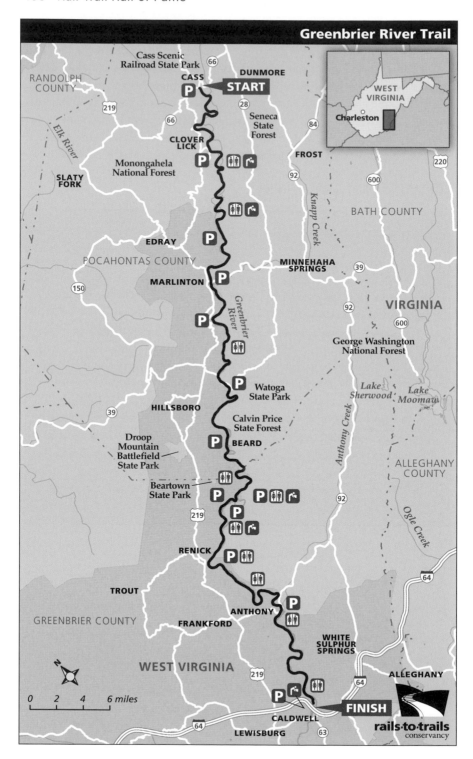

In a state with many fabulous rail-trails offering spectacular views and an abundance of natural wonders, the 77-mile-long Greenbrier River Trail (GRT) is the crown jewel of West Virginia's impressive trail selection. The gravel-surfaced route travels from Cass in the north to Caldwell in the south, following the Greenbrier River for most of the trip. Throughout the route, you will find yourself immersed in the serenity and solitude of this quiet corner of the state.

Begin at Cass Scenic Railroad State Park and enjoy a slight downhill slope on your route south. Cass draws large crowds for its spectacular train excursions. Located here is the world's largest fleet of geared Shay locomotives, including one turn-of-the-20th-century class C-80 Shay that has

The scenic route winds along the Greenbrier River.

Counties
Greenbrier, Pocahontas

Endpoints
Deer Creek Road near Back Mountain Road (Cass Scenic Railroad State Park in Cass) to Stonehouse Road near I-64 (North Caldwell)

Mileage
77.0

Roughness Index
2

Surface
Gravel

been traveling its route for almost 100 years. Follow the Greenbrier River and take advantage of the many opportunities to jump in for a quick cooldown or just wander along the riverbank. This is a popular fishing spot for smallmouth bass, and you are likely to see many people along the banks as you travel.

About 20 miles along is the town of Marlinton, which offers the perfect rest stop with several trailside restaurants. As you approach town, see the only remaining water tank from the former railway. Built in 1923, this tank has been restored. Here you will also find the remains of a railway turntable about 50 feet from the trail. Farther south in Watoga, at milepost 48 (the mile markers begin at the southern end of the trail), see the ruins of an old company store, the only reminder that this was once a booming logging town in the early 1900s. Other traces of the route's past you will come across include two dramatic tunnels and railroad bridges, as well as numerous whistle posts and historical mile markers.

As you travel the GRT, look for some of the colorful native flowering plants, such as common joe-pye, wild columbine, black-eyed Susan, and fall phlox, as well as for some of the numerous native and transient birds, such as yellow-throated warblers, northern flickers, and ruby-throated hummingbirds. You will find several campsites and additional trailheads as you continue south, but no other towns. This section is popular with horseback riders, however, so be cautious when approaching horses. The trail ends in Caldwell, where there is a parking area and water fountain.

RAIL-TRAIL HALL OF FAME SELECTION

The Greenbrier River Trail travels through one of the most beautiful and remote areas of West Virginia as it follows alongside its namesake river. In 2000 the trail was designated as one of only 52 Millennium Legacy Trails in the country in recognition of its significance; the trails were selected by the White House Millennium Council in partnership with Rails-to-Trails Conservancy, the U.S. Department of Transportation, the National Endowment for the Arts, and the American Hiking Society. Rich in wildlife and railroad history, this is one of the country's premier rail-trails, joining the Hall of Fame ranks in 2012.

RAILROAD HISTORY

Back in the late 1800s, the Chesapeake & Ohio Railway built a rail line along the Greenbrier River in order to haul timber. Later, the route became a vital link for passenger service between the Midwest and the East Coast. For nearly 100 years, this line carried passengers and freight, before finally being discontinued in 1978. While the route has seen a new life as the longest rail-trail in the state of West Virginia, many of the small towns that served the timber trade are long gone or a fraction of the size they were in their heyday.

On the route's northern end, the trailhead in Cass offers a welcoming start to the trail.

CONTACT: greenbrierrailtrailstatepark.com

DIRECTIONS

Trailheads are available in Caldwell, Cass, and Marlinton, as well as at several other locations along the route.

To reach the northern trailhead at Cass, take I-64 to Exit 169/Lewisburg. Follow US 219 60.4 miles north to WV 66 E. Turn right onto WV 66/Back Mountain Road, and go 2.3 miles. The trailhead will be on your right, just off Deer Creek Road. Or take WV 28 to WV 66 W, and look for the trailhead just off WV 66 on your left after 5.2 miles.

To reach the southern trailhead at North Caldwell, take I-64 E to Exit 175/US 60. Turn left (west) onto US 60, and go 2.7 miles to County Road 38/Stonehouse Road. The trailhead will be on your right in 1.4 miles. If you're coming from I-64 W, take Exit 169 to US 219; travel north 0.5 mile to CR 30/Brush Road, and turn right. From here, drive another 0.5 mile to CR 38/Stonehouse Road. The trailhead will be on the left in 3 miles.

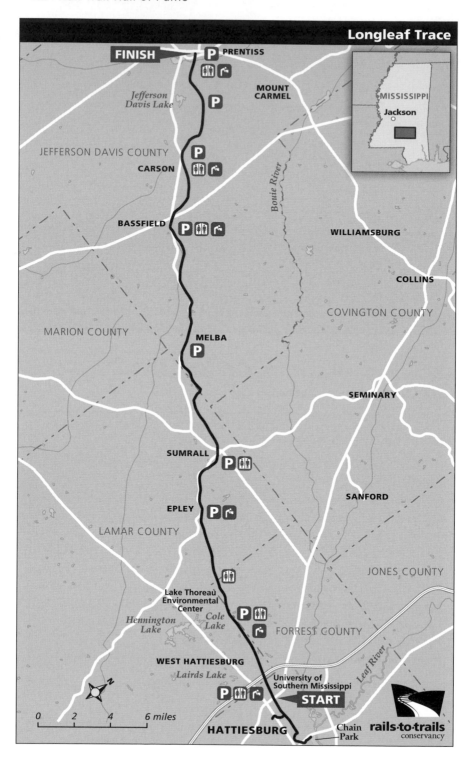

Longleaf Trace

FINISH

PRENTISS

Jefferson Davis Lake

MOUNT CARMEL

MISSISSIPPI

Jackson

JEFFERSON DAVIS COUNTY

CARSON

Bouie River

WILLIAMSBURG

BASSFIELD

COLLINS

COVINGTON COUNTY

MARION COUNTY

MELBA

SEMINARY

SUMRALL

SANFORD

EPLEY

LAMAR COUNTY

JONES COUNTY

Lake Thoreau Environmental Center

Hennington Lake

Cole Lake

FORREST COUNTY

Leaf River

WEST HATTIESBURG

Lairds Lake

University of Southern Mississippi

START

N

0   2   4   6 miles

HATTIESBURG

Chain Park

rails·to·trails
conservancy

With the scent of honeysuckle and wisteria permeating the air and beautiful flowering dogwood and magnolia trees lining the route, it is easy to glide along on the paved Longleaf Trace rail-trail without even realizing that 44 miles have passed by. Traveling a corridor between Hattiesburg and the small town of Prentiss, the route is named for the longleaf pine that once flourished in dense forests in the area. Heavily logged in the early part of the 20th century, the recovering woodlands today feature a variety of pine species, as well as flowering shrubs and other native plants.

Begin at the University of Southern Mississippi in Hattiesburg to have access to the trailhead's parking, restrooms, and drinking water. Visitors can also pick up a plant identification guide and a bike rental at the welcome

Long, straight stretches of the Longleaf Trace are popular with local cyclists.

Counties
Forrest, Jefferson Davis, Lamar

Endpoints
E. Eighth St. and Chain Park Dr. in Chain Park (Hattiesburg) to Columbia Ave. and Front St. (Prentiss)

Mileage
44.0

Roughness Index
1

Surface
Asphalt

A charming trailhead greets travelers at the northern end of the trail in Prentiss.

center. If you prefer, you could begin 1.9 miles farther east in historical downtown Hattiesburg, but note that there are no amenities at that trail terminus. A 2018 extension of 0.85 mile from the Hattiesburg Train Depot to Chain Park in northeast Hattiesburg provides another option for a quick exploration into nature. The 37-acre park provides relaxing green space along the Leaf River and includes a playground and restrooms.

Traveling northwest from the Southern Miss campus, you'll pass through a variety of landscapes rich in flora and fauna, while crossing several bridges and traversing tunnels. Keep your eyes open for some of the common tree species, such as loblolly pine, southern magnolia, mimosa, sassafras, white oak, and crabapple—and, of course, the longleaf pine, which can grow more than 100 feet, live more than 400 years, and is vital to the region's ecosystem due to the species' resistance to fire. Use a plant identification guide to locate various native plants, and take note of the many species that are identified for you with large labels. Also see wildlife, such as deer, wild hare, an assortment of bird species, and a scenic trailside beaver pond.

About 4 miles along, at the intersection with Jackson Road, take a 0.25-mile detour to visit the Lake Thoreau Environmental Center. Run by the University of Southern Mississippi, this facility includes miles of walking trails through a longleaf pine savanna. Fifteen miles farther along the rail-trail, keep alert for horses, as an equestrian path begins in Epley and crisscrosses the trail for the next 25 miles.

The Longleaf Trace is a very tranquil, shaded, and well-maintained route, but do remain cautious at several road crossings and be prepared for a slight uphill grade. The corridor has several covered rest areas and trailside amenities (including vending machines), along with such quirky trailside sites as a year-round decorated Christmas tree, a tank, and a llama farm. The route also passes through the small towns of Melba, Bassfield, and Carson, which all offer services, before arriving in Prentiss.

RAIL-TRAIL HALL OF FAME SELECTION

Inducted into the Hall of Fame in 2010, the Longleaf Trace is the longest rail-trail in the state and offers a well-maintained recreational corridor that immerses trail users in the serene beauty of southern Mississippi's pine forests. With trailside opportunities to learn more about the flora and fauna of this unique ecosystem, the route provides the perfect outdoor adventure.

RAILROAD HISTORY

The Longleaf Trace was once the corridor of the Mississippi Central Railroad, which built the route in the late 1800s to service the region's booming timber industry. The railroad was prosperous until the 1920s, during which time it covered more than 150 miles throughout the state. As the timber industry continued to decline, the route was sold to the Illinois Central in the 1960s. By the 1980s, the rail line was facing financial difficulties and, with decreasing usage, eventually discontinued operations between Hattiesburg and Prentiss.

CONTACT: longleaftrace.org

DIRECTIONS

To reach the Hattiesburg trailhead: Take I-59 to Exit 65 (Hardy St.) and head east 0.3 mile. Following the brown trail signs, turn left onto 38th Ave., and go 0.7 mile. Turn right at the next light onto Fourth St. Just past the M. M. Roberts Stadium, in 0.9 mile, turn left into the trailhead parking lot.

To reach the Prentiss trailhead: From Hattiesburg, take US 49 about 26 miles northwest to Collins, and turn west onto US 84. Go 18.7 miles, and exit onto MS 13/MS 184 toward Prentiss. Turn left (south) onto MS 13, and in 0.4 mile take a slight right onto Columbia Ave. Continue 0.9 mile to a four-way stop sign at Front St.; turn left and immediately see the trailhead parking lot situated in a park.

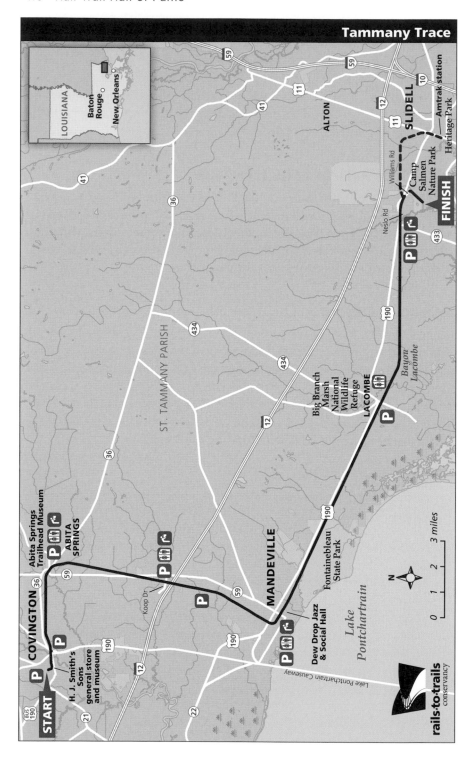

Louisiana's Tammany Trace is a Southern belle nestled in the pristine natural surroundings of the Northshore across vast Lake Pontchartrain from vibrant New Orleans. Spanning just over 28 miles, the rail-trail crosses a number of small creeks and bayous on more than two dozen bridges, connecting five quaint towns—Covington, Abita Springs, Mandeville, Lacombe, and Slidell—each with its own unique character and appeal.

In the tall piney woods, coastal marshes, and wetlands along the route, quiet travelers may have the fortune of seeing wild turkeys, red foxes, deer, rabbits, or even a wild boar or alligator. This lush backdrop has been a summer escape for New Orleans residents and other visitors since the early 1900s. Offering the best of both worlds, the Trace

The rail-trail winds through the piney woods and moss-draped oaks of St. Tammany Parish.

County
St. Tammany Parish

Endpoints
N. Theard St. and 26th Ave. (Covington) and Neslo Road, just south of US 190 W/Gause Blvd. (Slidell)

Mileage
28.2

Roughness Index
1

Surface
Asphalt

A bridge over Bayou Lacombe is one of the highlights of the Tammany Trace.

has many areas that feel remote, even though restaurants and shops are always close at hand. The Trace is such a smoothly paved, easy experience that the local bike shops primarily offer cruisers for rent. Horseback riding is also available on a parallel equestrian trail. A handful of trailheads, each only a few miles apart, offer convenient places to find parking, restrooms, and drinking water.

Begin your journey on the trail's western end in Covington, and be sure to peek into H. J. Smith's Sons general store and museum for a glimpse into the town's past; this local treasure has been family owned and operated since 1876. The trailhead in Covington, designed to resemble an old-fashioned railroad station, hosts a visitor center.

From Covington, it's a 3.4-mile ride to downtown Abita Springs, where travelers can enjoy restaurants and art galleries. Stop in at the Abita Springs Trailhead Museum for a history lesson on the town, long known for its nearby medicinal springs, and check out the two-story 1880s pavilion in the adjacent park.

From Abita Springs, the trail continues south 4.4 miles to the main trailhead on Koop Drive, where visitors will be greeted by staff working inside a green caboose. An inclusive playground, called Kids Konnection, also makes this a popular stop for families.

Continue south 4.3 miles to Mandeville, where a renovated train station serves as a trailhead and as a home to a cultural interpretive center. Come on a Saturday and you'll find the place abuzz with a community market of food and crafts. Nearby, you'll also find an amphitheater, which offers seasonal concerts, and a splash pad for the kids. Jazz once bloomed here, and just blocks from the trail is the historical Dew Drop Jazz & Social Hall, where legends like Louis Armstrong played in the early 1900s.

Beyond Mandeville, you'll come within several blocks of Lake Pontchartrain before angling inland. A worthwhile side trip here is the 2,800-acre Fontainebleau State Park, which hugs the shoreline. Visitors will find the brick ruins of an 1829 sugar mill here, and the park also has camping facilities and a pier over the lake—the perfect setting to take in a sunset.

A 9.1-mile journey takes you from Mandeville to Lacombe, a gateway to the sprawling Big Branch Marsh National Wildlife Refuge, where there are plentiful recreational opportunities, including hiking, bird-watching, and paddling. If you have extra time, rent a kayak or fishing gear to explore the scenic Bayou Lacombe from a different perspective. About a mile off the trail, the Bayou Lacombe Visitor Center features interactive exhibits about this incredible habitat, as well as a botanical garden to wander.

The trail once ended at the Slidell trailhead on Neslo Road, 5.8 miles beyond Lacombe. However, in early 2020, a new section was added to extend the Tammany Trace 1.2 miles to the picturesque Camp Salmen Nature Park, which offers a covered pavilion, a playground, an amphitheater, and other amenities. This new segment includes a short section of on-road riding on a residential street, Williams Road. Trail advocates hope to have the trail extended another 3 miles to Slidell's Heritage Park by late 2020. Nestled against the Bayou Bonfouca, the park offers a boat dock, picnic tables, and other facilities for outdoor fun.

RAIL-TRAIL HALL OF FAME SELECTION

The Tammany Trace provides an important legacy for Louisiana as the state's first rail-trail. Nationally, it was also one of the first rail-trails in the country supported by a landmark federal program called the Intermodal Surface Transportation Efficiency Act. Enacted in 1991, the legislation made it possible for federal transportation money to support walking and biking projects. In 2000 the Trace was designated as one of only 52 Millennium Legacy Trails in the country in recognition of its significance; the trails were selected by the White House Millennium Council in partnership with Rails-to-Trails Conservancy, the U.S. Department of Transportation, the National Endowment for the Arts, and the American Hiking Society. In 2017 the Trace entered the Rail-Trail Hall of Fame.

RAILROAD HISTORY

The history of the Tammany Trace is rooted in the parish's lumber and resort industries. The New Orleans & Northeastern Railroad came to St. Tammany

Parish in 1883. The line changed hands a few times over the years, and its final owner, Illinois Central Railroad, had ceased operations on the right-of-way by the late 1980s. The St. Tammany Parish government purchased the corridor in 1992, and the rail-trail's first section opened in 1994.

CONTACT: tammanytrace.org

DIRECTIONS

Parking, restrooms, and drinking water are available at the trailheads in Covington, Abita Springs, Mandeville, and Slidell-Carollo. In Lacombe, parking is just a short distance (0.9 mile) northwest of the trailhead.

To reach the western trailhead in Covington (419 N. New Hampshire St.) from I-12 E, take Exit 63B for US 190 W to Covington. Continue on US 190 for 3 miles to Covington. Turn left onto US 190 Bus. to head into town. Drive 0.5 mile, and turn right onto New Hampshire St. In 0.1 mile, you'll see the trailhead parking lot on your left.

To reach the main trailhead on Koop Dr. (where the trail office is housed inside a green caboose), from I-12 E, take Exit 65 for LA 59 N to Abita Springs. Take LA 59 N for 0.2 mile, and turn left onto Koop Dr. In 0.2 mile, you'll reach the trailhead parking area.

To reach the eastern trailhead in Slidell (2289 W. Gause Blvd.), from I-12, take Exit 80 for Northshore Blvd. (Airport Road). Once on Northshore Blvd., head south 1 mile. Turn right onto US 190 (Gause Blvd.). Travel 0.4 mile west on the highway, and turn left into the parking lot when you see the green PARK & RIDE sign.

For those who wish to arrive by train, Slidell offers an Amtrak station (1827 Front St.), located 4.6 miles from the eastern end of the trail. The station is serviced by Amtrak's *Crescent* line, which has connections in major cities such as New York City; Philadelphia; Washington, D.C.; Atlanta; and New Orleans.

One of the longest rail-trails in Mississippi, the Tanglefoot Trail meanders for 43.6 miles through lush backdrops and friendly communities in the foothills of the Appalachian Mountains in the Mississippi Hills National Heritage Area. The trail follows a former railroad line created by Col. William C. Falkner—great-grandfather of Nobel Prize–winning author William Faulkner (who added the *u* to the name)—in the late 1800s to connect his plantation interests in Mississippi to the Memphis and Charleston Railroad in Tennessee. Falkner's line eventually became part of the Gulf, Mobile & Ohio Railroad (GM&O), which hosted important freight and passenger trains on a corridor connecting St. Louis and the Gulf of Mexico.

The GM&O Rails-to-Trails Recreational District of North Mississippi was formed in 2006 and named the Tanglefoot Trail after one of the original train engines. The rail-trail opened in 2013.

A 2019 inductee into the Rail-Trail Hall of Fame, the Tanglefoot Trail is known for its lush and stunning backdrops.

Counties
Chickasaw, Pontotoc, Union

Endpoints
Daniel Boone St. and W. Church St. (Houston) and W. Bankhead St. and N. Railroad Ave. (New Albany)

Mileage
43.6

Roughness Index
1

Surface
Asphalt

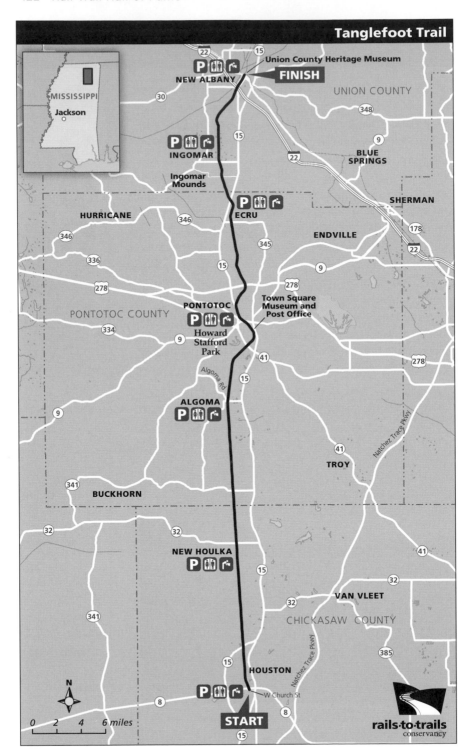

Tanglefoot Trail

MISSISSIPPI

Jackson

NEW ALBANY

Union County Heritage Museum

FINISH

UNION COUNTY

INGOMAR

Ingomar Mounds

BLUE SPRINGS

SHERMAN

HURRICANE

ECRU

ENDVILLE

PONTOTOC COUNTY

PONTOTOC

Howard Stafford Park

Town Square Museum and Post Office

ALGOMA

TROY

BUCKHORN

NEW HOULKA

VAN VLEET

CHICKASAW COUNTY

HOUSTON

W Church St

START

N

0   2   4   6 miles

rails·to·trails
conservancy

First traveled by American Indians, the trail's original corridor was also traced by famed explorers Hernando de Soto and Meriwether Lewis. The route was called the King's Highway after the last Chickasaw king, Ishtehotopah, who made his home near the creek where the trail crosses.

As the trail winds through three counties—Chickasaw, Pontotoc, and Union—it features mature hardwood forests, trees draped in kudzu, fields of cotton and soybeans, pastures, and wetlands. Dotted with spots to take refuge from the heat, the trail takes riders over wooden bridges that offer views of waterways and wildlife.

Along the way, the asphalt pathway connects six communities—Houston, New Houlka, Algoma, Pontotoc, Ecru, and New Albany—which offer pleasant places to rest, eat, and shop.

Four whistle-stops—reminiscent of train depots—serve as additional trail entrances and tributes to the pathway's rich history as a railroad. Located in New Houlka, Algoma, Ecru, and Ingomar, these trailheads provide restrooms, parking, water fountains, bike racks, electrical hookups, and picnic tables.

Beginning at the Houston trailhead on West Church Street, the route heads over MS 8 and then passes through a suburban area, followed by large swaths of woods and farmland on a 10-mile route to New Houlka. Another mostly tree-lined 15 miles take you through the region's expansive agricultural lands to Algoma at mile 20, and then to Pontotoc, where a gateway at about 25.4 miles provides water, restrooms, parking, and an event pavilion.

In Pontotoc, drop by the Town Square Museum and Post Office—from the gateway, go 0.3 mile east on West Reynolds Street, and then turn right onto North Main Street and go 0.2 mile south—to learn more about the lives of settlers during the construction of the railroad.

Just 2.5 miles west of the trail, you can access Howard Stafford Park, a city-owned facility with beautiful lake views and a range of recreational amenities and camping accommodations, including for those traveling by RV. To reach the park, head west on Reynolds Street for 0.8 mile; turn left onto MS 15, and go south for 0.1 mile; and then turn right onto Spur Street. Go 0.2 mile, and turn left onto MS 9. Go south for 0.6 mile, and then turn left onto Lake Drive. Go 0.6 mile, and you'll reach the park and parking lot, which is surrounded on three sides by Howard Stafford Lake. (The park is not on a designated bike route.)

The final leg of the trip takes you north through Ecru to Ingomar and then to the trail's northern terminus at the trailhead in New Albany. At the Ingomar whistle-stop, head south on County Road 96 for 1.2 miles and then west (right) onto CR 90 for 1.1 miles to visit the Ingomar Mounds, a Mississippi mound site and burial area dating back 2,200 years. (The mounds are not on a designated bike route.)

The Tanglefoot Trail winds through three counties and six communities in the foothills of the Appalachian Mountains.

In New Albany, trail users may wish to take in some regional cultural history at the Union County Heritage Museum (closed Sunday and Monday; go to **ucheritagemuseum.com** for details). It is accessible from the trailhead (near Main Street) by crossing West Bankhead Street, heading north on North Railroad Avenue for 0.1 mile, and then heading east (turn right) on Cleveland Street for 0.1 mile.

Of note, the Tanglefoot Trail sits between two historical sites from the life of an iconic American: Elvis Presley. His birthplace of Tupelo is about 25 miles east of the trail, and his Graceland estate is 90 miles northwest in Memphis. The rags-to-riches contrast between the two homes will be of interest to history buffs and rock 'n' roll lovers who visit the rail-trail and want to explore the surrounding area.

RAIL-TRAIL HALL OF FAME SELECTION

The Tanglefoot Trail was chosen by public vote among three nominees in 2019—receiving over 14,000 votes. One of Mississippi's longest rail-trails, the Tanglefoot's excellently maintained pathway and rich history are evident along its route, which connects three counties and six communities while providing access to a remarkable Mississippi landscape and delivering abundant economic, transportation, and health benefits to the region.

RAILROAD HISTORY

The Tanglefoot Trail preserves a disused piece of railroad corridor assembled in part for the Gulf and Ship Island Railroad (G&SI), which was launched by Col. William C. Falkner in 1872. Originally called the Ripley Railroad Company—and subsequently the Ship Island, Ripley and Kentucky Railroad Company—the line was initially intended to connect Ripley, Mississippi, with Middleton, Tennessee, but would later be part of Col. Falkner's vision for a railroad connecting all the way from the Great Lakes to the Gulf of Mexico. The line was extended to New Albany and then to Pontotoc by 1888, after which it was renamed the G&SI.

In 1889 Falkner was shot by his former partner, R. J. Thurmond, after a business dispute, and his properties were sold by his son and combined into the Gulf and Chicago Railroad. The line was sold to the Mobile, Jackson and Kansas City Railroad in 1902 and extended to Houston, Mississippi, by 1906. A series of name changes, reorganizations, and mergers followed—with the line eventually stretching 2,800 miles and connecting the Gulf of Mexico to the Great Lakes, 76 years after it was first launched by Col. Falkner.

CONTACT: tanglefoottrail.com

DIRECTIONS

To reach the southern trailhead in Houston from I-22, take Exit 85 for the Natchez Trace Pkwy., and turn left. Go 24.8 miles, and take the MS 32 exit. Turn right onto MS 32 W, and go 4.7 miles. Turn left onto MS 15 S, and go 2.1 miles. Turn left onto County Road 515 N/Old Hwy. 15, go 0.1 mile, and take a slight right to continue on CR 515 N/Old Hwy. 15. Go 1.5 miles, and continue onto Jackson St. Go 1.1 miles, take a slight right onto N. Pontotoc St., and go 0.7 mile. Turn right onto MS 8/W. Madison St., go 0.2 mile, and turn left at the first cross street onto Dr. M. L. King Jr. Dr. S. Go 0.1 mile, and turn right onto W. Church St. Go 0.1 mile, and look for parking at the trailhead on your left.

To reach the southern trailhead in Houston from MS 8/W. Madison St. heading west, turn south onto Pontotoc St. At the second intersection, turn right onto W. Church St. Go three blocks, and look for parking at the trailhead on your right.

To reach the midpoint gateway in Pontotoc from I-22/US 78 E, take Exit 64 for MS 15/MS 30 E toward Pontotoc/Ripley. Turn right (south) onto MS 15, and go 15.8 miles. Turn left onto W. Reynolds St., and go 0.8 mile. Parking is located at the Pontotoc Gas System Warehouse at 140 W. Reynolds St. To access the midpoint gateway from W. Reynolds St. heading west, take a right onto S. College St. and then an immediate left into the trailhead parking lot.

To reach the northern trailhead in New Albany from I-22, take Exit 63 toward Downtown/New Albany. If heading west, turn right onto Carter Ave. If heading east, turn left onto Bratton Road, and then immediately continue onto Carter Ave. Go 0.9 mile, and turn right onto W. Main St. Go 400 feet, and turn right onto King St. Take an immediate right into the parking lot at the Union County Library. The northern endpoint is less than 500 feet farther north along the trail.

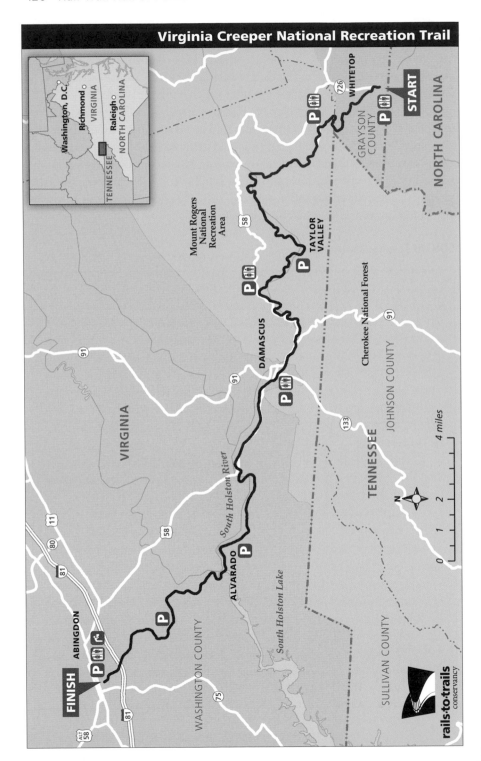

Virginia Creeper National Recreation Trail

27 Virginia Creeper National Recreation Trail

Nestled in the southwest corner of Virginia, you'll find the bucolic Virginia Creeper Trail (VCT). Stretching almost 33 miles from near the North Carolina border through wooded areas, rolling farmland, and charming small towns, the trail follows the former corridor of a steep mountain railroad, a train that had to creep up a nearly 7 percent grade. Today, the remnants of the former railroad, in the form of numerous bridges and restored trailside railcars and engines, combined with stunning scenery, make this one of the most popular rail-trails in the state.

The best place to start the VCT in order to take advantage of the descents is at the highest point at Whitetop Station. The trailhead here, which is actually about 1 mile from the eastern endpoint, has a visitor center as well as amenities. Note that there are several bike shops in Damascus, and one in Abingdon, that will provide shuttle

The western half of the trail between Damascus and Abingdon is open and pastoral.

Counties
Grayson, Washington

Endpoints
Whitetop Station Visitor Center on Whitetop Gap Road near Dolinger Road/VA 653 (Whitetop) to Green Spring Road at Gibson St. SE (Abingdon)

Mileage
32.7

Roughness Index
2

Surface
Gravel

services to the trailhead, a good option if you are looking to avoid the uphill grade or want to ride the trail one way.

From the beginning, enjoy stellar views as you travel through the dense forest of Mount Rogers National Recreation Area. Look for deer, cottontail rabbits, and grouse, and, although rare, possibly spot a black bear. Periodically, you may also find hikers crossing your path as the Appalachian Trail weaves its way through the area. Depending on the season, see beautiful flowering plants, such as rhododendron, redbud, wild cherry, and fields of colorful wildflowers.

About 18 miles along is the town of Damascus, also known as Trail Town USA due to the convergence here of the VCT, the Appalachian Trail, US Bicycle Route 76, and the Iron Mountain Trail. Find shops and restaurants catering to trail users, and stop by the visitor center in a restored caboose.

Farther along, experience a different landscape, as the trail crosses a large trestle that towers above the South Holston River and later meanders through wide valleys and pastoral farmland. This section has a gradual incline and possibly bumpy conditions because of the popularity of horseback riding. Keep in mind that most of the VCT goes through private land. This will be especially apparent south of Abingdon where you find cattle gates across the trail. In town, stop to explore the historic district and visit *Mollie,* a steam engine dating back to 1907, which now proudly marks the trailhead of the VCT.

RAIL-TRAIL HALL OF FAME SELECTION

Given the huge economic impact that the VCT has had on the small towns of Abingdon and Damascus, it's hard to believe that the trail almost didn't materialize. Initially met with a lot of opposition from landowners, the 33-mile trail—officially opened in 1987—has since become a much-loved destination and a boon for economic development. Today, the towns welcome about 250,000 riders per year, more than 25 times their combined populations, and tens of millions of dollars are generated annually in spending for rentals, lodging, food, beverages, and other trail-user needs for the businesses along the route. Joining the Hall of Fame in 2014, the route is a great example of how rail-trails can invigorate communities.

RAILROAD HISTORY

Constructed in the late 1800s by the Virginia–Carolina Railroad, the original route went from Abingdon to Damascus and was later extended by the Norfolk and Western Railroad to North Carolina to haul lumber, iron ore, supplies, and passengers. The route included about 100 trestles and bridges, sharp curves, and steep grades. Crews faced significant challenges, including washouts and rockslides, trying to keep the mountain railroad in operation. The Great

The pathway offers dozens of picturesque trestles.

Depression was the beginning of the end for the line, although it limped along for years, with the last train eventually running in 1977.

CONTACT: vacreepertrail.org

DIRECTIONS

To get to the Whitetop trailhead, take I-81 to Exit 19 (Abingdon/Damascus). Turn right (east) and follow US 58 for 10.7 miles into Damascus. Continue on US 58 by turning right and following it another 16.4 miles. Turn right onto VA 726/Whitetop Gap Road, and head south toward the North Carolina border. After 1.5 miles, you will see the parking area off VA 726.

To get to the Abingdon trailhead, take I-81 to Exit 17. Head north on US 58 Alt./Cummings St. for 0.2 mile. Turn right onto Green Spring Road, and follow it 0.5 mile. A large locomotive engine is on display by the trailhead, which you can see across from the parking lot.

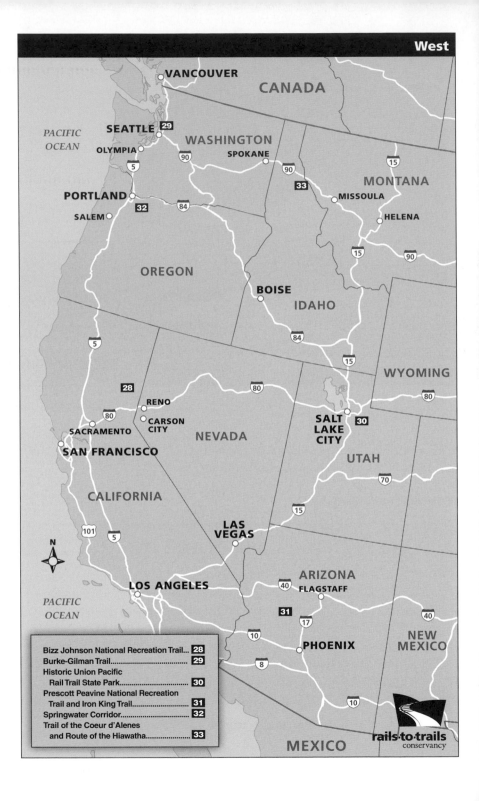

VANCOUVER

CANADA

*PACIFIC
OCEAN*

SEATTLE **29**

OLYMPIA

WASHINGTON

SPOKANE

5

90

90

15

MONTANA

33

MISSOULA

HELENA

PORTLAND

32

84

SALEM

15

90

OREGON

BOISE

IDAHO

84

15

WYOMING

5

80

80

28

RENO

80

CARSON
CITY

SACRAMENTO

SAN FRANCISCO

NEVADA

SALT
LAKE
CITY

30

UTAH

70

CALIFORNIA

101

5

LAS
VEGAS

15

N

LOS ANGELES

40

ARIZONA

FLAGSTAFF

*PACIFIC
OCEAN*

31

17

40

NEW
MEXICO

10

PHOENIX

8

10

Bizz Johnson National Recreation Trail... **28**
Burke-Gilman Trail.. **29**
Historic Union Pacific
   Rail Trail State Park.................................. **30**
Prescott Peavine National Recreation
   Trail and Iron King Trail........................... **31**
Springwater Corridor.................................. **32**
Trail of the Coeur d'Alenes
   and Route of the Hiawatha...................... **33**

MEXICO

rails·to·trails
conservancy

WEST

Arizona's Prescott Peavine National Recreation Trail skirts Watson Lake, which features dramatic rock formations (see page 144).

Bizz Johnson National Recreation Trail

Named after former Congressman Harold T. "Bizz" Johnson, who was instrumental in its establishment, the 25-plus-mile Bizz Johnson Trail (BJT) travels through a remote and stunningly beautiful area of northeastern California. The trail follows the Susan River as it winds through a rugged canyon, crossing the river 12 times and passing through two tunnels. This high-elevation trail is a combination of semiarid canyon and upland ever-green forests and offers spectacular scenery, especially in autumn when the foliage is breathtaking.

The BJT follows an old logging route, and while the grade is not overly steep, the best way to tackle the trail is to begin in Westwood in order to enjoy the downhill. In a nod to the town's long history in the timber industry, look for a 25-foot carved redwood statue of Paul Bunyan and Babe the Blue Ox at the trailhead.

Upland forests of pine and fir line the path.

County
Lassen

Endpoints
Mason Station on County Road A-21, 3.3 miles north of CA 36 (Westwood), and Susanville Railroad Depot at Richmond Road and Cypress St. (Susanville)

Mileage
25.4

Roughness Index
2

Surface
Dirt, Gravel

The trail's two tunnels are highlights of the route.

Here, find thick pine-scented forests home to American kestrels and great horned owls. As the trail descends, pass through different landscapes, including oak woodlands, high desert, and grasslands, before reaching the Susan River. Follow the river—lined by picturesque boulder fields, meadows, and basalt cliffs—for the remaining 16 miles. This is a popular spot for anglers hoping to hook a rainbow trout, as well as campers, and it attracts wildlife, such as beavers, muskrats, porcupines, coyotes, and even black bears. Enjoy dramatic scenery and relics from the railroad's past in the form of bridges, trestles, and tunnels that are scattered all along this section of the route. Also keep alert for horseback riders, who frequent the BJT.

This is a rural rail-trail and, other than the trailheads at either end, the BJT does not pass through any towns. Be prepared and bring plenty of water, food, and anything else needed for the day. The route has a number of benches and scenic spots where you can stop for a picnic lunch, as well as easy access for a quick dip in the river on hot days. Mountain bikers will enjoy opportunities to connect to other trails, including the South Side Trail, which provides a challenging singletrack. Also note that the Bizz Johnson Marathon, a Boston Marathon qualifier, takes place here in October, so plan accordingly.

The BJT ends in Susanville, with an old caboose marking the trailhead. Here, you can visit the Susanville Railroad Depot, which serves as a historical museum and visitor center for the region's trails. From Susanville, it is possible to take a public bus back to Westwood. The bus drops passengers off at the intersection of CA 36 and County Road A-21; from here, you can bike about 3 miles to the trailhead.

RAIL-TRAIL HALL OF FAME SELECTION

Featuring spectacular rural scenery, the BJT is truly a route that immerses travelers in their surroundings. Joining the Hall of Fame in 2008, this high-elevation rail-trail is one of the few places in the state of California to experience four distinct seasons, making it a popular destination year-round.

RAILROAD HISTORY

The BJT follows the route of the Fernley and Lassen Branch Line of the Southern Pacific Railroad. This route began operations in 1914, carrying lumber, and a limited number of passengers, from Westwood to Fernley, Nevada. Lumber was transported until 1952, after which time passenger service continued until 1956. After a flood destroyed a major bridge, the structure was never repaired, and the section of the route from Westwood to Susanville fell into disuse, although the line east of Susanville remained active until 1979.

CONTACT: blm.gov/visit/bizz-johnson or
lassenlandandtrailstrust.org/bizz-johnson-trail

DIRECTIONS

To reach the western end of the trail: From Reno, Nevada, take US 395 north for 80.6 miles. Continue straight on CA 36 for 25.6 miles to Westwood, and turn right (north) onto County Road A-21. Continue 3.3 miles to CR 101/McCoy Road (just before the railroad tracks). Follow CR 101 for 0.5 mile until you reach the Mason Station trailhead. The station has ample parking.

To reach the Susanville Railroad Depot on the eastern end of the trail: From Reno, Nevada, take US 395 north for 80.6 miles. Continue 4.5 miles on CA 36, which becomes Main St. in Susanville. Follow Main St. through Historic Uptown Susanville to Weatherlow St., at the base of the hill. Turn left (south) onto S. Weatherlow St. (which becomes Richmond Road), and continue 0.5 mile to the Susanville Railroad Depot Trailhead Visitor Center, where you can park.

Burke-Gilman Trail

From its beginning along the banks of the majestic Puget Sound, through vibrant Seattle neighborhoods, along the shoreline of beautiful Lake Washington, to its endpoint in the suburb of Bothell, the Burke-Gilman Trail ("The Burke") delivers a true Pacific Northwest experience.

Since it was built in the 1970s, the route has helped set the standard for urban trails, combining a functional link to neighborhoods and attractions with a well-loved recreational trail. The Burke-Gilman Trail is also a host trail for the 3,700-plus-mile Great American Rail-Trail, which will one day form a seamless connection between Washington, D.C., and Washington State.

Begin at Golden Gardens Park and travel along the waterfront to reach historical Ballard Locks. Opened in 1917, the locks link Puget Sound with Lake Union and Lake Washington. Stop to watch boats travel through this well-used locks system and, if here during spawning season, head to the viewing area across the canal to watch

Gas Works Park is a unique attraction along the route.

County
King

Endpoints
Golden Gardens Park
at Seaview Ave. NW
(Seattle) to 102nd Ave.
NE near Woodinville Dr./
WA 522 (Bothell)

Mileage
18.8

Roughness Index
1

Surface
Asphalt

The trail is an important commuter corridor, connecting popular destinations across the city.

salmon navigating the ladder (spawning season varies by species). Created so that the fish could travel upstream to spawn, the ladder contains 21 steps, or weirs, allowing the fish to navigate around the locks. This side of the canal is also home to the Carl S. English Jr. Botanical Garden, a wonderful park to wander through and see native plant specimens.

Back in Ballard, a break in the trail requires trail users to navigate a 1.5-mile section on road. To do this, when the trail ends at 30th Avenue, take a quick left turn to reach Northwest 54th Street, then turn right onto 54th, and bear right onto Northwest Market Street. Take the third right onto Shilshole Avenue, and immediately after traveling under the Ballard Bridge, bear left onto Northwest 45th Street to pick up the trail again at 11th Avenue Northwest and 45th Street.

As you continue along the Burke, pass through the colorful Fremont neighborhood, with its numerous shops and restaurants, before reaching Gas Works Park. Listed on the National Register of Historic Places, the park contains what remains of a coal gasification plant that operated 1906–1956. Today the site is a local landmark due to its quirky, artful repurposing of the old plant. Next, travel around the campus of the University of Washington and follow the shoreline of Lake Washington north. Along the way, enjoy spectacular views and pass lakefront parks, including Matthews Beach Park, the city's largest freshwater swimming beach.

The Burke skirts along the north end of Lake Washington before arriving in Blyth Park in Bothell. For those looking for a longer ride, make a seamless transition here to the 11-mile Sammamish River Trail.

RAIL-TRAIL HALL OF FAME SELECTION

One of America's first rail-trails, built in the 1970s, the Burke-Gilman Trail has become a major active transportation artery for Seattle. The route connects to employment centers, hospital facilities, major cultural destinations, and neighborhoods, as well as to the University of Washington, making it a prime commuter pathway. Inducted into the Hall of Fame in 2008, it's also a hugely popular recreational corridor, with beautiful Mount Rainier visible in the distance.

RAILROAD HISTORY

Created in 1885 by Thomas Burke and Daniel Gilman, the Seattle, Lake Shore and Eastern Railway once claimed this corridor as its own. The railroad was established in an effort for the city of Seattle to become a transportation center, and plans were to ultimately connect with the Canadian Pacific Railway. While the route never got that far, it did become an important regional line serving the Puget Sound logging areas. In 1901 the railway was purchased by the Northern Pacific Railroad and was used by the logging industry through 1963, eventually becoming inactive in 1971.

CONTACT: seattle.gov/parks/burkegilman/bgtrail.htm or **burkegilmantrail.org**

DIRECTIONS

To reach Golden Gardens Park from I-5, take Exit 172 to N. 85th St., and head west 3.4 miles to 32nd Ave. NW. Turn right onto 32nd Ave. NW, and continue on Golden Gardens Dr. NW for 0.8 mile. Turn left onto Seaview Pl. NW, which meets Seaview Ave. NW and a parking lot in 0.2 mile. Disability parking is available.

To reach Blyth Park from I-405, take Exit 23 to WA 522 W toward Seattle. After 0.2 mile, bear right onto Kaysner Way. Turn left onto Main St. After 0.1 mile, turn left onto 102nd Ave. NE. When the road ends at 0.3 mile, turn right onto W. Riverside Dr. Blyth Park is 0.5 mile ahead.

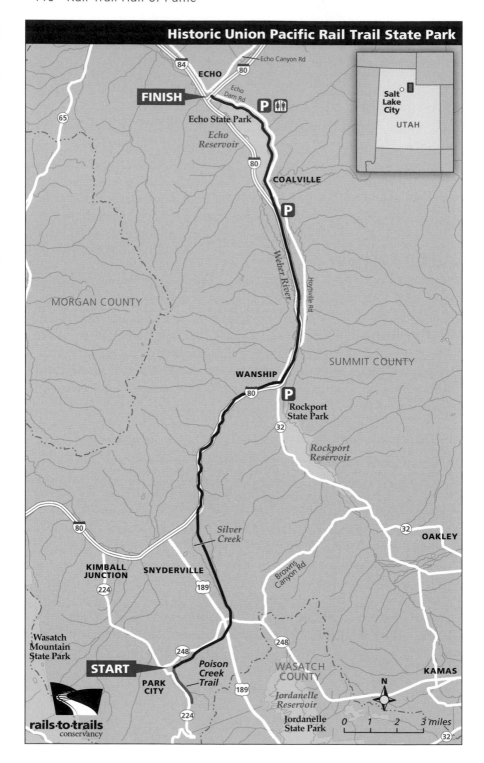

Historic Union Pacific Rail Trail State Park

84
ECHO
80
Echo Canyon Rd

FINISH
Echo Dam Rd
P 🚻

Echo State Park

Echo Reservoir

65

80

COALVILLE

P

Weber River

Hoytsville Rd

MORGAN COUNTY

SUMMIT COUNTY

WANSHIP
80
P
Rockport State Park
32

Rockport Reservoir

32   **OAKLEY**

Browns Canyon Rd

Silver Creek

KIMBALL JUNCTION   SNYDERVILLE
224
189

248   248

Poison Creek Trail
START
PARK CITY
189
WASATCH COUNTY
KAMAS

Wasatch Mountain State Park

224

Jordanelle Reservoir

N

Jordanelle State Park

0   1   2   3 miles

32

Salt Lake City
UTAH

rails·to·trails
conservancy

UTAH

30 Historic Union Pacific Rail Trail State Park

Experience one of the crown jewels of the Park City area, the 28-mile Historic Union Pacific Rail Trail (HUP). Traversing its namesake state park, the trail offers stunning views of the Wasatch Mountain Range as it travels across wetlands in Silver Creek Canyon, through small towns, and along Weber River to Echo Reservoir. As you bike, stop to read the 16 plaques scattered along the trail, which provide interesting facts and stories about the early Mormon settlers, the prehistoric animals that once roamed these parts, and the coal and silver industries that were the lifeblood of the area in the late 1800s.

From Park City, the trail begins at an elevation of 6,900 feet and descends at a 2 percent grade for the first 14 miles. Enjoy this gradual descent and take in the surrounding

County
Summit

Endpoints
Poison Creek Trail at Bonanza and Iron Horse Drs. (Park City) to Echo Dam Road near I-80 (Echo Reservoir, Coalville)

Mileage
28.0

Roughness Index
1–2

Surface
Asphalt, Gravel

The trail offers stunning views of the Wasatch Mountain Range as the path traverses the Silver Creek Canyon.

Surrounded by mountains, Coalville, along the northern end of the trail, offers spectacular views.

mountain views. Note that the first 3 miles of the route are paved, before turning to gravel. Travel along Silver Creek for 14 miles through a narrow volcanic canyon, where you may spot some of the wildlife that thrives in this area, including bald eagles, herons, moose, and foxes. The trail follows I-80 before reaching Wanship, where the route meets up with the Weber River, which flows between Echo Reservoir and Rockport Reservoir. This river is popular with fishermen, and you are likely to spot anglers as you travel along.

Next, continue through historic Coalville. Established in 1850 by Mormon settlers, this town struck prosperity in 1859 when challenged by the territorial government in Utah to find coal within 40 miles of Salt Lake City for a reward of $1,000. A coal vein was discovered and mining took off, eventually transforming the entire area. See remnants of the town's heyday in the form of several architecturally significant buildings that are located along Main Street, which provides a nice detour through this small town. Only a few miles past Coalville, the path ends at the western mouth of Echo Canyon. The last several miles, however, offer stunning scenery as you ride alongside Echo Reservoir.

RAIL-TRAIL HALL OF FAME SELECTION

In addition to offering visitors stunning panoramic mountain scenery, the HUP is rich in history. Trailside plaques allow visitors to gain a better appreciation for the people and events that shaped the towns along the route, while the trail showcases a startlingly beautiful landscape that draws people from all over the world. This trail joined the Hall of Fame in 2010.

RAILROAD HISTORY

The corridor the HUP follows was first carved out in 1871 when part of the present-day route was used by the Summit County Railroad Company to transport coal from Coalville mines to the Wasatch Front. Once silver was discovered in Park City, the Utah Eastern Railroad and the Echo-Park City Railway both completed lines to bring coal in to fuel the pumps that removed water from underground mines and to transport silver out to reach the Union Pacific transcontinental line passing through Echo. Both lines were completed in 1880 and were vital to the booming silver-mining industry, which saw Park City grow into a prosperous western town.

CONTACT: stateparks.utah.gov/parks/historic-union-pacific-rail-trail

DIRECTIONS

To reach the southern trailhead in Park City: Take I-80 to Exit 146 for US 40 E/US 189 S. After 3 miles, take Exit 4 (for Park City) and take a right onto UT 248 W/Kearns Blvd. After traveling west on Kearns for 2.6 miles, turn left onto Bonanza Dr., and look for the trailhead just past Munchkin Road. Parking is available on side streets.

To reach the northern trailhead at Echo Reservoir in Echo State Park (2115 N. Echo Dam Road, Coalville, UT 84017): From I-80 in Echo, take Exit 169 and turn left (under the decorative orange bridge) onto Echo Dam Road. Continue south 2.2 miles until you see the parking lot on your right (a $6 parking fee applies).

Trailheads are also available in Wanship and Coalville, and access is available at several other locations along the route.

Prescott Peavine National Recreation Trail and Iron King Trail

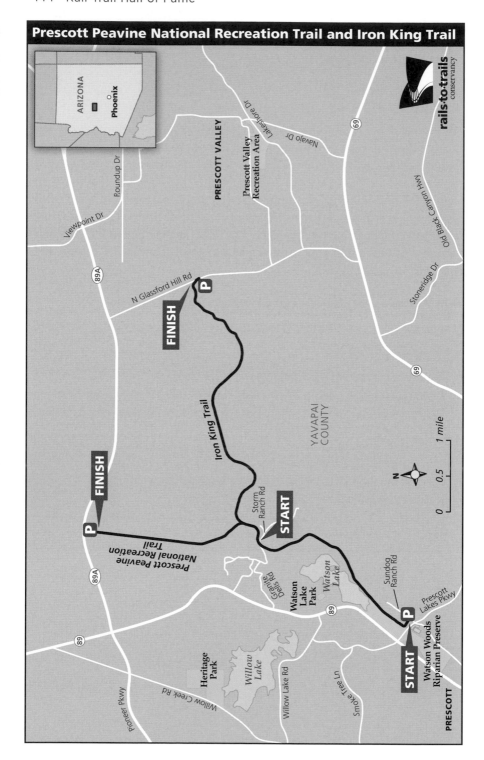

Incredible views are the hallmark of the 6-mile Prescott Peavine National Recreation Trail and the 4.1-mile Iron King Trail. Located just outside Prescott, Arizona, at an elevation of 5,200 feet, the combined route skirts the southern end of stunning Watson Lake, features dramatic giant rock mounds known as the Granite Dells, and contains fascinating reminders of the corridor's railroad past. The rugged terrain is best suited for mountain bikes; horseback riders can also use the entire length of the Peavine Trail, but not the Iron King Trail.

Begin at the southern end of the Prescott Peavine Trail about 4 miles north of Prescott. Near the trailhead, find the 126-acre Watson Woods Riparian Preserve. What visitors

The Iron King Trail has a distinctly western beauty.

County
Yavapai

Endpoints
Prescott Peavine Trail: North of Prescott Lakes Pkwy. at AZ 89 to south of AZ 89A at Side Road (Prescott); Iron King Trail: Prescott Peavine Trail near Storm Ranch Road (Prescott) to N. Glassford Hill Road at Santa Fe Loop Road (Prescott Valley)

Mileage
10.1 combined (Prescott Peavine Trail: 6.0; Iron King Trail: 4.1)

Roughness Index
2

Surface
Prescott Peavine Trail: Ballast, Cinder, Crushed Stone, Dirt; Iron King Trail: Dirt

The Granite Dells are a highlight of the Prescott Peavine National Recreation Trail.

see today is all that remains of what was once a 1,000-acre riparian forest of cottonwood and willow trees. Decimated by decades of livestock grazing, sand and gravel extracting, and firewood cutting, the area has seen a resurgence of vegetation and wildlife and offers a verdant oasis in an otherwise stark landscape.

Once on the trail, skirt the southeastern portion of Watson Lake. This area, as well as the preserve, is a top birding spot, and hundreds of species—including eagles, pelicans, and great blue herons—flock here. The lake, surrounded by the spectacular Granite Dells, has crystal-clear water. This is a popular tourist attraction that features picture-postcard views of the lake, framed out by the enormous weather-beaten granite boulders, creating a surreal landscape. Spend time exploring the rocks to take in views from different vantage points, such as the stunning sight of Granite Mountain off in the distance.

Point of Rocks, at mile 3, provides a reminder of the route's past. The trail passes through a cut made by the railroad, which blasted through a cluster of tall granite spires in order to lay tracks. Beside the trail, find a historical marker that features an image from more than 100 years ago, showing an engine traversing the same pass. Shortly afterward, you'll reach a fork in the trail. Head left to reach the end of the Peavine Trail 1 mile farther along (note that this section passes through private property, so remain on the trail at all times). Turn right to join the Iron King Trail and head into a landscape of scraggly desert woods before reaching open desert, where the view stretches out for miles. See remnants of the railroad in the form of old train cars, which periodically appear trailside along the remainder of the route.

RAIL-TRAIL HALL OF FAME SELECTION

Joining the Hall of Fame together in 2010, the Prescott Peavine and Iron King Trails showcase the beautiful countryside outside Prescott and offer visitors a stunning varied landscape of verdant green, stark desert, dramatic geological formations, striking views, and fascinating relics from the route's railroad past.

RAILROAD HISTORY

The Prescott Peavine Trail follows the route carved by the former Santa Fe, Prescott & Phoenix Railway in 1893. The route was eventually acquired by the Atchison, Topeka & Santa Fe Railway and remained in service until 1983, when floods damaged trestles farther north. The Iron King's route was built by the Prescott and Eastern Railway in the late 1890s to service the Iron King and two other mines in the area. The route was folded into the Santa Fe and stayed prosperous through the 1920s before eventually falling out of use.

CONTACT: **prescott-az.gov/recreation-events/recreation-areas/trails** and **pvaz.net/182/prescott-valley-trails**

DIRECTIONS

To reach the southern trailhead of the Prescott Peavine Trail, from I-17, take Exit 278 for AZ 169. Head west on AZ 169, and go 15 miles. Turn right onto AZ 69, and head north 12.7 miles. Turn right onto Prescott Lakes Pkwy., and go 1.9 miles north to Sundog Ranch Road. Turn right and look for a large parking lot on the left. There is a $3 fee to park.

To reach the northern trailhead of the Prescott Peavine Trail, from I-17, take Exit 278 for AZ 169. Head west on AZ 169, and go 15 miles. Turn right onto AZ 69, and head north 2.4 miles. Turn right onto Fain Road, and follow it 7.2 miles. Merge onto Pioneer Pkwy./AZ 89A, and go 4.5 miles to Exit 319 for Granite Dells Pkwy. Continue on Granite Dells Pkwy. 0.3 mile, and take the first right onto Centerpointe East Dr. In 0.4 mile turn left onto Side Road. The trailhead will be on your left at the turn, and the parking lot is at the end of Side Road.

To reach the eastern end of the Iron King Trail in Granville, from I-17, take Exit 278 for AZ 169. Head west on AZ 169, and go 15 miles. Turn right onto AZ 69, and head north 7.6 miles. Turn right onto N. Glassford Hill Road, and go 1.8 miles to the intersection with Santa Fe Loop Road. The trail starts at a large dirt parking lot.

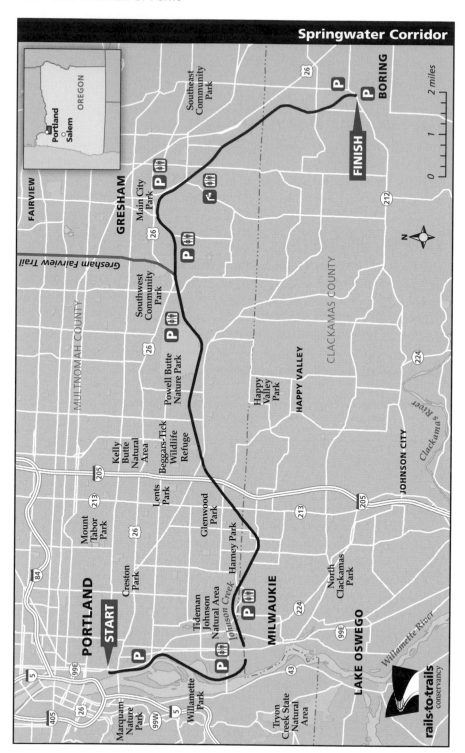

Springwater Corridor

Portland, Oregon, is a cyclist's dream, with a seemingly endless network of trails that travel throughout the city and into the suburbs. Of the many options, one of the most popular routes is the 21.5-mile Springwater Corridor (SC). Following the Willamette River, the trail heads in the direction of majestic Mount Hood, which tantalizingly beckons you from afar as you leave the city behind.

In 1904 the city of Portland invited the Olmsted Brothers architecture firm to develop a plan to beautify the city in preparation for the Lewis and Clark Centennial Exposition. Their proposal was a 40-mile interconnected system of parks surrounding the city. While this plan did not come to fruition exactly as envisioned, over time the loop took shape and today is about 140 miles long and connects more than 30 parks in an almost continuous

Visitors to the Springwater Corridor enjoy the sight of Mount Hood as they head out of town.

Counties
Clackamas, Multnomah

Endpoints
SE Fourth Ave. and SE Ivon St. (Portland) to Clackamas-Boring Hwy. No. 174/OR 212 and SE Richey Road (Boring)

Mileage
21.5

Roughness Index
1

Surface
Asphalt

Johnson Creek flows beside and below the Springwater Corridor.

route around the city, in addition to several far-reaching spurs. The SC is a major segment of this route.

Departing from Portland, the SC follows Willamette River before veering off to a short on-road section called the Sellwood Gap, spanning 2,100 feet. Turn left when the trail ends and follow Southeast Linn Street. Turn right onto Southeast 19th Avenue to rejoin the trail. After passing through a light industrial area, come upon Tideman Johnson Natural Area, the first of many green spaces on the route. For most of the way, the SC is intertwined with Johnson Creek, which it crosses several times.

About midway, the trail crosses under I-205. Equestrian use is most common east of I-205, where a separate soft-surface path meanders away from the main trail as topography allows. Along the eastern half of the trail, you will find Leach Botanical Garden, which features 2,000 plant species in its beautifully landscaped grounds. This garden is actually located 0.5 mile from the SC but is worth the side trip (turn right onto Southeast 122nd Avenue and follow to the entrance).

At the Linnemann Station trailhead, find the 3-mile-long Gresham Fairview Trail, which will eventually link to Marine Drive Trail, part of the trail loop encircling Portland. Farther along (at mile 16), travel through Gresham's Main City Park to reach a light transit station to return to downtown Portland. (To reach it: Head through the park and turn onto Main Avenue; follow the avenue north and turn right onto Northeast 10th Drive.) Keep your eyes on the horizon and experience the grandeur of Mount Hood, which is an arresting sight rising up in the distance. In the future, plans are to continue the SC to the mountain, but for now the trail ends 5 miles past Gresham in Boring.

RAIL-TRAIL HALL OF FAME SELECTION

The Springwater Corridor is a beautiful and serene route on its own, but combined with Portland's vast interconnected transportation network, it provides a vital link for thousands of commuter and recreational trail users every day. Joining the Hall of Fame in 2011, the route is a jewel in a region with many fabulous rail-trail options.

RAILROAD HISTORY

Known variously as the Portland Traction Company Line, the Cazadero Line, and the Bellrose Line, but ultimately called the Springwater Division Line, the route of the Springwater Corridor was built in the early 1900s to transport passengers, farm goods, and timber from areas south and east of Portland into the city. Original plans called for the route to travel to the town of Springwater, but that never materialized, although the name lingered. To encourage passenger use of the rail line, an amusement park was built along the route, but by 1958 passenger service ended, while freight service continued until 1989.

CONTACT: portlandoregon.gov/parks

DIRECTIONS

Access to the trail is available at many locations, including the I-205 Multi-Use Path.

To reach the Ivon St. trailhead in Portland, from I-5, take Exit 300B (US 26/OR 99E). Keep left, following signs for Oregon City, and then keep right, following signs for McLoughlin Blvd./US 26. Continue south on SE Martin Luther King Jr. Blvd., and go 0.8 mile. Take the exit toward SE Ivon St., and turn left. Park along the street.

To reach the Johnson Creek Blvd. trailhead, from I-205, take Exit 16 and go east on SE Johnson Creek Blvd. for 2.2 miles. Turn left to stay on Johnson Creek Blvd., and the trailhead is just past Johnson Creek on your right. To reach the Boring trailhead at 28000 SE Dee St., from Gresham, head west-southwest on US 26 for 3.8 miles. Turn left onto SE Stone Road, and after 0.5 mile, take a right onto SE 282nd Ave. Go 2 miles, and turn right onto OR 212. Take an immediate right onto SE Dee St., and parking will be on the left. From I-205, take Exit 14. Go east on SE Sunnyside Road for 5.8 miles. Turn left onto OR 212, and follow it 4.5 miles. Turn left onto SE Dee St., and parking will be on the left.

Other trailheads, including in Gresham, are located along the route.

Trail of the Coeur d'Alenes and Route of the Hiawatha

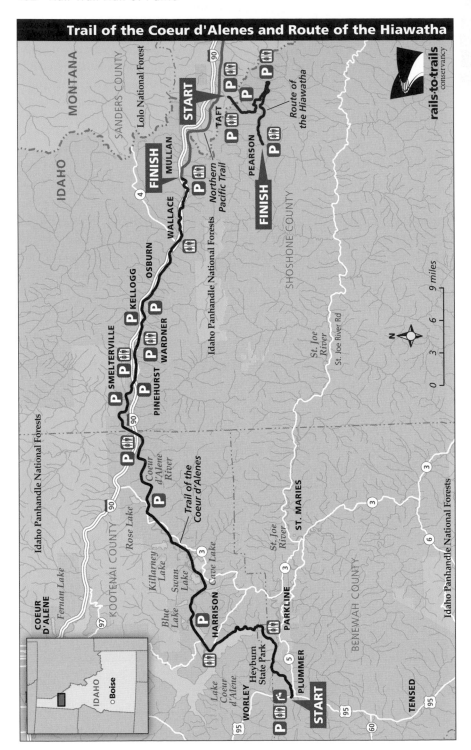

33 Trail of the Coeur d'Alenes and Route of the Hiawatha

GREAT
AMERICAN
RAIL-TRAIL

Offering two of the most distinctive and memorable rail-trail experiences in the country, the 73-mile Trail of the Coeur d'Alenes (TCA) and the 15-mile Route of the Hiawatha (RoH) showcase everything that is spectacular about the great state of Idaho. Each trail alone is worth a visit, but cyclists who choose to combine them can really immerse themselves in the region's natural beauty on a multiday riding adventure. And, while the trails are not connected, future plans include creating a 190-mile loop that is sure to excite rail-trail enthusiasts. The TCA is also a host trail for the 3,700-plus-mile Great American Rail-Trail, which will one day form a seamless connection between Washington, D.C., and Washington State.

Begin the TCA at the western trailhead in Plummer. At Heyburn State Park, the trail crosses Lake Coeur d'Alene on the Chatcolet Bridge. Follow the shoreline as you continue north and enjoy the expansive views of

The Route of the Hiawatha features seven high trestles.

Counties
TCA: Benewah, Kootenai, Shoshone; RoH: Shoshone

Endpoints
TCA: Anne Antelope Ave. at US 95 (Coeur d'Alene Tribe Veterans Memorial Park in Plummer) to River St. at Second St. (Mullan); RoH: East Portal of St. Paul Pass Tunnel (Montana–Idaho border in Taft, MT) to Moon Pass Road near Forest Service Road 300A (Pearson)

Mileage
88.0 combined
(TCA: 73.0; RoH: 15.0)

Roughness Index
1–2

Surface
TCA: Asphalt;
RoH: Gravel

the Palouse prairie before reaching the chain lakes region. Linked together by the Coeur d'Alene River, this area is home to diverse wildlife, such as coyotes, moose, and birds of prey. Afterward, enter the Silver Valley, one of the most productive silver-mining regions in the country. Along the route, pass through small towns offering amenities before reaching the trail's end in the mountain town of Mullan, near the Montana border. At the restored depot here, you can find a railroad museum, which is the only place on the TCA to learn more about the corridor's railroad past. Past Mullan, the Northern Pacific Trail (NorPac) begins, which continues east into Montana and includes a connection to the eastern end of the RoH.

The RoH is simply spectacular. This rail-trail features stunning mountain views from seven towering trestles and has 10 tunnels, including the 1.6-mile-long St. Paul Pass Tunnel, or Taft Tunnel. The tunnel, which burrows under the Bitterroot Mountains between Montana and Idaho, is a highlight of the trail for many. Take advantage of shuttle opportunities and begin the RoH at the East Portal to enjoy a downhill ride to Pearson, where the trail ends. From here, it is possible to bike farther on a rough, unofficial rail-trail, which will bring you within approximately 18 miles of the TCA. This is the route that will one day connect, completing the loop.

Note that the RoH is operated by Lookout Pass Ski Area under a special-use permit of the U.S. Forest Service and requires that trail users obtain and display a trail pass. Information about this, as well as rentals and shuttle services, can be found at the website below.

RAIL-TRAIL HALL OF FAME SELECTION

Joining the Hall of Fame in 2010, the Trail of the Coeur d'Alenes and Route of the Hiawatha offer more than 80 miles combined through some of the most remote and jaw-dropping scenery in the country. These rail-trails provide the ideal routes to experience the grandeur of Idaho.

RAILROAD HISTORY

For nearly 100 years, beginning just after the Civil War, the mighty Union Pacific Railroad traveled along the present-day route of the TCA, transporting silver, zinc, and lead. In 1907, beneath the Bitterroot Mountains where the RoH now travels, the Milwaukee Railroad began building a corridor in this forbidding terrain to reach the West Coast. After a number of devastating events, including a massive 1910 fire, the railroad continued operations but had only a handful of prosperous years before suspending service in 1961.

CONTACT: parksandrecreation.idaho.gov/parks/trail-coeur-d-alenes and ridethehiawatha.com

The Trail of the Coeur d'Alenes can be enjoyed in any season.

DIRECTIONS

The Route of the Hiawatha can be accessed from several trailheads.

To reach the East Portal of the St. Paul Pass Tunnel (in Montana): From I-90, take Exit 5 toward Taft. Follow signs to reach the trailhead 2 miles along. Begin by heading east 0.2 mile, and turn right at Randolph Creek. Take the next first right, and go 2 miles south. East Portal will be on the left.

To reach the trailhead in Pearson, from I-90, take Exit 61 toward Wallace. Turn right then left onto Front St., and go 0.2 mile. Turn right onto Second St., and in 0.3 mile, turn right onto Bank St. (which becomes King St.). In 0.5 mile King St. becomes Forest Service Road 456/Placer Creek Road; continue 7.2 miles. Turn left onto FS 16, and in 0.2 mile, turn right to stay on FS 16. In 1.1 miles, make a sharp left to turn onto Moon Pass Road/FS 456, and continue 9.8 miles.

The Trail of the Coeur d'Alenes has 19 trailheads along the route.

To reach the western trailhead in Plummer: From I-90, take Exit 12 for US 95. Head south on US 95 S, and in 0.8 mile, turn right to stay on US 95 S another 32.1 miles. Turn right onto Anne Antelope Ave. as you approach the town. Look for the parking lot and trailhead on your left.

To reach the eastern trailhead in Mullan: From I-90, take Exit 68, which leads to the I-90 Business loop through town. Almost immediately after exiting, take a left onto Second St., and then make an immediate right into the trail parking lot.

The fall colors along California's Bizz Johnson National Recreation Trail are spectacular (see page 132).

Index

A

Abita Springs Trailhead Museum (LA), 118

Alabama's Chief Ladiga Trail and Silver Comet Trail, 1, 100–103

Alden B. Dow Home & Studio (MI), 85, 87

Allen County Historical Society Museum (KS), 91

American Discovery Trail, 68

Antioch College, Yellow Springs (OH), 71

Appalachian Trail, 128

Arizona's Prescott Peavine National Recreation Trail and Iron King Trail, 131, 144–147

Atchison, Topeka & Santa Fe Railway, 89, 92

Atlanta Beltline (GA), 102

Atlantic Coast Line, 107

Audubon Nature Center and Aquarium (RI), 12

B

Ballard Locks, Seattle (WA), 137

Battle of Gettysburg (PA), 38, 40

Bayou Lacombe Visitor Center (LA), 119

Bedford Depot Park (MA), 34

Bellrose Line, 151

Benjamin Banneker Park (VA), 43

bicycles, 5, 6

Big Branch Marsh National Wildlife Refuge (LA), 119

Big Savage Tunnel (PA), 16

Bizz Johnson Marathon, 134

Bizz Johnson National Recreation Trail (CA), vi, 132–135

Black Hills (SD), 57, 59

Blue Ox Trail (MN), 83

book, how to use this, 3–5

Boston & Maine Railroad, 35

Brainerd & Northern Minnesota Railway, 84

Brainerd Lakes Area (MN), 81

Buck Creek Trail (OH), 71

Bunyan, Paul, 83, 133

Burke, Thomas, 139

Burke-Gilman Trail (WA), viii, 136–139

Burlington Northern Railway, 84

C

California's Bizz Johnson National Recreation Trail (BJT), vi, 132–135

Camp Salmen Nature Park (LA), 119

Canadian Pacific Railway, 139

Capital Trails Coalition (CTC), 2

Cardinal Greenway (IN), 48–52

Carl S. English Jr. Botanical Garden, Seattle (WA), 138

Casselman River, 16

Cass Scenic Railroad State Park (WV), 109, 110

Cazadero Line, 151

Cedar Lake LRT Regional Trail (MN), 75

Cedartown Depot (GA), 102

Chain of Lakes (MN), 75

Chelsea Market (NY), 20

Chelsea Thicket (NY), 21

Chesapeake & Ohio Canal Towpath, 17

Chesapeake & Ohio Railway (C&O), 52, 88, 110

Chicago, Aurora & Elgin Railroad, 64

Chicago, Indianapolis, & Louisville Railroad, 80

Chicago & North Western Railway, 56, 60

C (continued)

Chief Ladiga Trail and Silver Comet Trail (AL, GA), 1, 100–103
children, 7
Chippewa National Forest (MN), 83
Chippewa River, 85
Cincinnati, Richmond and Muncie Railroad (CR&M), 52
Civil War, 37, 38, 39, 40, 45, 80, 154
Coalville (UT), 142, 143
Coeur d'Alene River, 4, 154
Colchester Causeway (VT), 30
Crazy Horse Memorial (SD), 59
Creekside Trail (OH), 71
Crow Wing State Park, Brainerd (MN), 81
CSX Railroad, 103
Custer State Park (SD), 59
Cyrus E. Dallin Art Museum, Arlington (MA), 34

D

Dali Museum (FL), 105
Damascus (VA), 127
Deadwood (SD), 57, 59
de Soto, Hernando, 123
Dew Drop Jazz & Social Hall (LA), 119
dogs, 7
Dow, Herbert H., 87
Dow Gardens, Dow Historical Museum (MI), 87

E

East Bay Bike Path (RI), ix, 11–13
East trails, 8–45
Echo-Park City Railway, 143
Elroy-Sparta State Trail (WI), 1, 53–56
Empire State Trail, 23

F

Falcone Flyover (NY), 21
Falkner, Col. William C., 121, 124–125
Fernley and Lassen Branch, Southern Pacific Railroad, 135
Flint & Pere Marquette Railway, 88
Flint Hills Trail State Park (KS), 91
Florida's Fred Marquis Pinellas Trail (FMPT), 104–107
Fontainebleau State Park (LA), 119
Fort Ancient (OH), 71
Fred Marquis Pinellas Trail (FL), 104–107
Fred Meijer White Pine Trail State Park (MI), 88

G

Gas Works Park, Seattle (WA), 137, 138
George S. Mickelson Trail (SD), 57–60
Georgia's Silver Comet Trail, 100–103
Gettysburg Address, 38
Gilman, Daniel, 139
Glen Helen Nature Preserve (OH), 71
Golden Gardens Park (WA), 137
Graceland estate of Elvis Presley (MS), 124
Grand Island & Wyoming Central Railroad, 60
Granite Dells, Prescott Peavine National Recreation Trail (AZ), 146
Great Allegheny Passage (MD, PA), 14–17
Great American Rail-Trail, 3, 15, 49, 137, 153
Greenbrier River Trail (WV), 108–111
Gresham Fairview Trail (OR), 150
Gulf and Chicago Railroad, 125
Gulf and Ship Island Railroad (G&SI), 124–125
Gulf, Mobile & Ohio Railroad (GM&O), 121

H

Hall of Fame
  East trails, 8–45
  Midwest trails, 46–97
  overview map, iv
  South trails, 98–129
  West trails, 130–155
Heartland State Trail (MN), 83
Heritage Rail Trail County Park & Torrey
  C. Brown Rail Trail (MD, PA), 36–40
Heyburn State Park, Plummer (ID), 153
High Line (NY), 1, 18–21
Historic Union Pacific Rail Trail State
  Park (UT), 140–143
H. J. Smith's Sons general store and muse-
  um (LA), 118
Honeymoon Island State Park (FL), 106
Hopewell Depot (NY), 25
Howard Stafford Park, Pontotoc (MS),
  123
Howard Tunnel (PA), 38
Hudson River Railroad, 21
Hudson Valley Trail Network (NY), 1,
  22 27

I

icons
  map, 5
  trail use, 7
Idaho's Trail of the Coeur d'Alenes &
  Route of the Hiawatha, 4, 152–155
Illinois Central Railroad, 115, 119–120
Illinois Prairie Path, 1, 61–64
India Point Park, Providence (RI), 11
Indiana
  Cardinal Greenway, 48–52
  Monon Trail, 47, 77–80
Indianapolis Cultural Trail (IN), 79
Ingomar Mounds (MS), 123

Iowa's Wabash Trace Nature Trail, 93–97
Iron King Trail (AZ), 144–147
Iron Mountain Trail, 128
Island Line Rail Trail (VT), 28–31

J

Jacksonville State University (GA), 101
John Chesnut Sr. Park (FL), 106
John C. Rudy County Park (PA), 37, 39
Johnson, Congressman Harold T. "Bizz,"
  133

K

Kabekona River, 83
Kansas's Prairie Spirit Trail State Park,
  89–92
Katy Trail State Park (MO), 1, 65–68
Kendall Depot (WI), 55
Kenilworth Trail (MN), 75

L

Lake Bemidji State Park (MN), 83
Lake Calhoun (MN), 75
Lake Champlain (VT), 29, 30, 31
Lake Coeur d'Alene (ID), 153–154
Lake Manawa Trail (IA), 95
Lake of the Isles (MN), 75
Lake Pontchartrain (LA), 117
Lake Shore and Eastern Railway, 139
Lake Tarpon (FL), 106
Lake Thoreau Environmental Center
  (MS), 114
Leach Botanical Gardens (OR), 150
Leavenworth, Lawrence, & Fort Gibson
  Railroad, 92
Lewis, Meriwether, 123
Lewis and Clark National Historic Trail
  (IL), 67–68
Lexington Depot (MA), 34

L (continued)

Lincoln, Abraham, 38
Lincoln Marsh Natural Area (IL), 63
Little Miami Railroad (LMRR), 72
Little Miami River, 69, 71
Little Miami Scenic Trail (OH), 69–72
Loess Hills (IA), 95
Longleaf Trace (MS), 112–115
Looff, Charles I. D., 12
Looff carousel, Crescent Park (RI), 12
Louisiana's Tammany Trace, 116–120

M

Mandeville (LA), 118–119
maps. *See also specific rail-trail*
    East trails, 8
    Hall of Fame trails, iv
    icons, 5
    Midwest trails, 46
    overall, regional locator, detailed trail, 5
    South trails, 98
    West trails, 130
Marais Des Cygnes River, 91
Marine Drive Trail (OR), 150
Marlinton (WV), 110
Marott Park (IN), 79
Martin Olav Sabo Bridge (MN), 75
Maryland
    Great Allegheny Passage (GAP), 14–17
    Torrey C. Brown Rail Trail (TCB) and Heritage Rail Trail County Park (HRT), 36–40
Massachusetts's Minuteman Commuter Bikeway, 32–35
Matthews Beach Park, Seattle (WA), 138
Mickelson, Governor George S., 57
Michigan's Pere Marquette Rail-Trail (PMRT), 85–88
Midland Trace Trail (IN), 79
Midtown Greenway (MN), 73–76
Midwest trails, 46–97
Millennium Legacy Trail, 68, 110, 115
Milwaukee Railroad, 76, 154

Minnesota
    Midtown Greenway, 73–76
    Paul Bunyan State Trail (PBST), 81–84
Minuteman Commuter Bikeway (MA), 32–35
Mississippi
    Longleaf Trace, 112–115
    Tanglefoot Trace, 121–125
Mississippi Central Railroad, 115
Mississippi Hills National Heritage Area, 121
Mississippi River, 75
Missouri River, 65
Missouri-Kansas-Texas Railroad, 68
Missouri's Katy Trail State Park, 1, 65–68
Mobile, Jackson and Kansas City Railroad, 125
Monkton Train Station (MD), 37
Monongahela River, 15
Monon Trail (IN), 47, 77–80
Morgan Lake Park (NY), 25
Mount Rogers National Recreational Area (VA), 128
Muncie (IN), 50–51
Museum of Fine Arts (FL), 105

N

New Orleans & Northeastern Railroad, 119–120
New York
    High Line, 1, 18–21
    Hudson Valley Trail Network, 1, 22–27
New York, New Haven & Hartford Railroad, 12, 25, 26
Norfolk and Western Railroad, 96, 128
Northern Central Railroad, 39
Northern Central Railroad Trail (MD), 37
Northern Pacific Railroad, 139
Northern Pacific Trail (NorPac), 154

O

Ohio's Little Miami Scenic Trail, 69–72
Old Depot Museum (KS), 88

Oregon's Springwater Corridor (SC), 148–151

P

Park City (UT), 141, 143
Paul Bunyan State Trail (MN), 81–84
Pennsylvania
    Great Allegheny Passage, 14–17
    Torrey C. Brown Rail Trail (TCB)
      and Heritage Rail Trail County Park (MD, PA), 36–40
Pequot Lakes (MN), 83
Pere Marquette Rail-Trail (MI), 85–88
Pine Haven Recreation Area (MI), 87
Pinkerton Tunnel (PA), 16
Pittsburgh and Lake Erie Railroad (P&LE), 17
Pittsburgh, Cincinnati & St. Louis Railway, 72
Point State Park, Pittsburgh (PA), 15
Portland (OR), 149
Portland Traction Company Line, 151
Pottawatomie Creek, 91
Prairie Grass Trail (OH), 71
Prairie Spirit Trail State Park (KS), 89–92
Prescott and Eastern Railway, 147
Prescott Peavine National Recreation Trail & Iron King Trail (AZ), 131, 144–147
Preseault v. United States, 30
Presley, Elvis, 124
Providence River, 12
Pumpkinvine Depot, Trestle (GA), 102

R

Railbanking Act of 1968, 30
Rails-to-Trails Conservancy (RTC), iii, vii
railstotrails.org, iii
rail-trails, 1–2
rail-with-trails, 2
ratings, trail, 5
Rhode Island's East Bay Bike Path (EBBP), ix, 1, 11–13
Route of the Hiawatha (ID), 152–155
Rutland-Canadian Railroad, 30

S

Salisbury Viaduct (PA), 16
Sammamish River Trail (WA), 139
Sanford Centennial Museum (MI), 87
Santa Fe, Prescott & Phoenix Railway, 147
Seaboard Air Line, 107
Seattle (WA), 137
Shingobee Connection Trail (MN), 83
Silver Comet Trail (GA), 100–103
Silver Creek Canyon (UT), 141, 142
Simon Kenton Trail (OH), 71
Slidell's Heritage Park (LA), 119
South Dakota's George S. Mickelson Trail, 57–60
Southern Pacific Railroad, 135
South Holston River, 128
South trails, 98–129
Southwind Rail Trail (KS), 91
Sponge Docks (FL), 106
Springwater Corridor (OR), 148–151
Springwater Division Line, 151
St. Paul Pass Tunnel (ID), 154
Steam into History excursion train (PA), 38
Summit County Railroad Company, 143
Susan River (CA), 133, 134
Susanville Railroad Depot (CA), 135
Sweetser Switch Trail (IN), 50

T

Taft Tunnel (ID), 154
Talladega National Forest (AL), 101–102
Tammany Trace (LA), 116–120
Tanglefoot Trail (MS), 121–125
Tarpon Springs (FL), 106
Thurmond, R. J., 125
Tideman Johnson Natural Area, 150
Tittabawassee River, 85
Tony Williams Park (NY), 23–24
Torrey C. Brown Rail Trail & Heritage Rail Trail County Park (MD, PA), 36–40
Trail of the Coeur d'Alenes and Route of the Hiawatha (ID), 4, 152–155
Trail Town USA (VA), 128

T *(continued)*

TrailLink.com trail-finder website, iii, 6, 7
TrailNation, trailnation.org, 2
trails. *See also specific trail*
  descriptions, 5–6
  East, 8–45
  Hall of Fame (map), iv
  Midwest, 46–97
  ratings, 3
  roughness index rating, 5
  South, 98–129
  trail use icons, 7
  use, 6–7
  West, 130–155

U

Uncle Sam Memorial Statue (MA), 34
Union County Heritage Museum (MS),
  124
Union Pacific Railroad, 154
University of Southern Mississippi,
  Hattiesburg, 113, 114
US Bicycle Route 76, 128
Utah Eastern Railroad, 143
Utah Eastern University, 128
Utah's Historic Union Pacific Rail Trail
  State Park (HUP), 140–143

V

Valley View Trail (IA), 95
Vermont's Island Line Rail Trail (ILRT),
  28–31
Veterans Memorial Park (MI), 87
Village Park, Sanford (MI), 87
Virginia Creeper National Recreation
  Trail, x, 99, 126–129
Virginia's Washington & Old Dominion
  Railroad Regional Park (W&OD), 41–45
Virginia-Carolina Railroad, 128

W

Wabash Railroad, 96
Wabash Trace Corridor (IA), 96

Wabash Trace Nature Trail Marathon
  (IA), 93
Wabash Trace Nature Trail (IA), 93–97
Walkway Over the Hudson, 23
Walkway Over the Hudson State Historic
  Park, 24, 25, 26
Washington & Old Dominion Railroad
  Regional Park (VA), 41–45
Washington's Burke-Gilman Trail, viii,
  136–139
Watoga (WV), 110
Watson Lake (AZ), 131, 146
Watson Woods Riparian Preserve (AZ),
  145
Watts, May Theilgaard, 61
Weber River, 142
Western Maryland Scenic Railroad, 9,
  16–17, 17
West River Parkway Trail (MN), 75
West trails, 130–155
West Virginia's Greenbrier River Trail
  (GRT), 108–111
Whitetop Station (VA), 127
Whitewater Gorge Trail (IN), 51
Whitney Museum of American Art, New
  York City, 20
Whittemore Park (MA), 34
Willamette River, 149, 150
William R. Steinhaus Dutchess Rail Trail,
  23, 25, 26
Winooski River Bridge (VT), 30
Wisconsin's Elroy-Sparta State Trail, 1,
  53–56
Wysor Street Depot, Muncie (IN), 51

X

Xenia-Jamestown Connector Trail (OH),
  71

Y

Yellow Springs Bridge (OH), 69
Youghiogheny River, 16

One of the most dramatic features of Minnesota's Midtown Greenway (see page 73) is the Martin Olav Sabo Bridge.

Photo Credits

Support Rails-to-Trails Conservancy

The nation's leader in helping communities transform unused rail lines and connecting corridors into multiuse trails, Rails-to-Trails Conservancy (RTC) depends on the support of its members and donors to create access to healthy outdoor experiences.

Your donation will help support programs and services that have helped put more than 24,000 rail-trail miles on the ground. Every day, RTC provides vital assistance to communities to develop and maintain trails throughout the country. In addition, RTC advocates for trail-friendly policies, promotes the benefits of rail-trails, and defends rail-trail laws in the courts.

Join online at **railstotrails.org,** or mail your donation to Rails-to-Trails Conservancy, 2121 Ward Court NW, Fifth Floor, Washington, D.C. 20037.

Rails-to-Trails Conservancy is a 501(c)(3) nonprofit organization, and contributions are tax deductible.

A highlight of Idaho's Trail of the Coeur d'Alenes is a series of mountain lakes (see page 152).

Find your next trail
adventure on TrailLink

Visit TrailLink.com today.

TrailLink
by Rails-to-Trails Conservancy